SPECIAL EDUCATIONAL NEEDS

THE BASICS

D0024387

'This well written introductory book offers trainee and experienced teachers a very useful and broad introduction to a complex field.'
Brahm Norwich, *Professor of Educational Psychology and Special Educational Needs, University of Exeter, UK*

Providing an engaging and complete overview, *Special Educational Needs: The Basics* examines the fundamental principles of the subject from policy to practice, covering:

- the historical development of special provision and key legislation
- identification and assessment of young people's special learning and behaviour needs
- working with a wide range of individual difficulties in practice
- the personal experiences of individuals with special needs
- special needs provision and the children's workforce.

This book is an ideal starting point for all those with questions about what constitutes special educational needs and how individuals can be supported in practice. It is also an essential reading for trainees, teachers and all others working with young people who experience difficulties in learning and behaviour, or who have special sensory or physical needs.

Janice Wearmouth is the Professor of Education at the University of Bedfordshire, UK, and has extensive experience of working in the area of special educational needs and inclusion.

The Basics

SPECIAL EDUCATIONAL NEEDS

THE BASICS

Janice Wearmouth

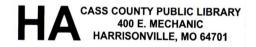

Routledge
Taylor & Francis Group

LONDON AND NEW YORK

First published 2012
by Routledge
2 Park Square, Milton Park, Abingdon, Oxon OX14 4RN

Simultaneously published in the USA and Canada
by Routledge
711 Third Avenue, New York, NY 10017

Routledge is an imprint of the Taylor & Francis Group, an informa business

British Library Cataloguing in Publication Data
A catalogue record for this book is available from the British Library

Library of Congress Cataloging in Publication Data
Wearmouth, Janice.
Special educational needs, the basics / Janice Wearmouth.
p. cm.—(The basics)
Includes bibliographical references.
1. Special education—Great Britain. 2. Children with disabilities—Education—Great Britain. 3. Mainstreaming in education—Great Britain. I. Title.
LC3986.G7W43 2012
371.90941—dc23
2011022084

ISBN 978-0-415-59223-9 (hbk)
ISBN 978-0-415-59224-6 (pbk)
ISBN 978-0-203-15518-9 (ebk)

Typeset in Aldus and Scala Sans
by Book Now Ltd, London

Printed and bound in Great Britain by
TJ International Ltd, Padstow, Cornwall

This book is for Chris and Hannah,
with lots of love and all good wishes for the future.

CONTENTS

FIGURES

ACKNOWLEDGEMENTS

I would like to thank Widgit for their kind permission to reproduce examples of Widgit Symbols and symbols from the Makaton Vocabulary Development Project.

INTRODUCTION

FRAMES OF REFERENCE: SPECIAL EDUCATIONAL NEEDS, LEARNING AND BEHAVIOUR

Over time, a number of frames of reference – that is, ways of looking at and interpreting what is around us – have been developed and become important in the world of special educational needs (SEN). It is important to recognise these and have a grasp of how they are used in order to understand SEN policy, practice and provision. This chapter includes a discussion of frames of reference that are very commonly used in schools in relation to SEN, children's learning and behaviour. It also includes a brief discussion of different ways in which the 'needs' of each child can be viewed in relation to the difficulty that is experienced and what they imply about the individual learners so described.

A number of pen portraits of young people who experience different kinds of difficulties in learning and behaviour serve to illustrate some of these frames of reference.

A problem-solving approach to address needs that can be very effective in overcoming barriers to learning is discussed.

DISCOURSES ASSOCIATED WITH SPECIAL EDUCATIONAL NEEDS, LEARNING AND BEHAVIOUR

In schools, the expression 'special educational needs' refers to difficulties in learning that require special educational provision. We might ask ourselves whether the frame of reference we use to judge the learning and behaviour of children identified as having 'special educational needs' enables us to understand these children in the same way as others. These days, with inclusion in schools and society in such high focus, the practical consequences of our answer to this question are very important for us all. We might illustrate this point with reference to 'James' whose dyslexic difficulties were misinterpreted as one point in his education as slowness in learning for which an appropriate response was withdrawal from the mainstream classroom and tuition with other 'slow learners'. Fortunately for him other teachers later on took a different view. They recognised that here was a young man who, in circumstances where people listened to him, could be articulate and, apart from difficulties in literacy acquisition, very able.

DISCOURSES AROUND DIFFICULTIES IN LITERACY AND THEIR CONSEQUENCES

A few years ago, 'James, aged 21, graduated with an Upper Second Honours degree from a well-known English university. He went on to study for his Masters degree. He had clearly become academically very successful with very high expectations of himself. High expectations of him by others was not always the case, however.'

In his primary school, aged 9 'James' was placed in the lowest ability groups for reading and writing in his class and withdrawn for special lessons on account of serious difficulties in literacy acquisition.

'. . . first of all, when I went to the lessons, I was called out in front of the class, and they were referred to as special lessons, and politically correct as the teacher thought that was, it really wasn't. Kids are cruel, and I felt really targeted and singled out.'

He was clearly dyslexic, as later assessment by an educational psychologist confirmed. Dyslexia was not a label that was recognised in James's local education authority at that time, however. Separation from competent literacy learners in the classroom and tuition in low-level 'remedial' literacy activities that he felt were irrelevant and meaningless resulted in feelings of hopelessness, helplessness and frustration. Great feelings of defiance and frustration resulted from the conflict between the provision made by the school, what he felt he needed, and by his own impotence in the situation:

'. . . the lessons that they gave seemed very simple. They were like obvious repetitive stuff, going over stuff that I found simple … I think the type of work that it was, was perhaps, writing out a page of like, a hundred, you know a full page worth of say a letter at a time, say D, repeating it over and over again and although my hand writing wasn't fantastic, I could write the letter D, but then that seemed to bear no relation to me writing a word.'

The category of 'slow learner' had been created in that school in order to manage special literacy provision, and hovered in the air ready to 'gobble up' likely candidates such as James (Meehan, 1996).

James' experiences in secondary school were very different, however. There he was encouraged to see himself as capable of making sense of his own world. Teachers responded to his difficulties in a way that suited his individual learning needs and they engaged in two-way discussion with him about the best ways to address his learning needs. With the added motivation of teachers expecting that he could learn, despite extreme tiredness every day James began to look for ways to achieve and overcome his difficulties:

'I became very strategic … it was a strategy I worked out for myself [that] seemed blatantly obvious. If the course provides a syllabus, and the examiners can only ask you on that syllabus, then why not learn everything in the syllabus, and keep to that? Basically for the sciences, I could get a book, and just work through each point of the syllabus, and if I knew it then … I didn't almost need the lessons…. I basically listed each point of the syllabus, and found the relevant piece of information and picked it out… '

Self-taught study skills, supported by sensitive, aware teachers who responded to James' initiatives and a growing sense of personal agency enabled James to achieve success at the General Certificate of Secondary Education level (GCSE):

'. . . before then it was blips … But when I did my GCSEs, I think all told I took thirteen, I got two A stars, six As five Bs. By then people were like, 'Bloody hell!' and then it got to my A-levels, and in the three sciences I got three B grades which was quite good.'

These skills, refined for study at degree level, enabled James to extend responsibility for his own learning until his graduation.
(Adapted from Wearmouth, 2004a, pp 60–67)

WHAT DOES THE LABEL 'SPECIAL EDUCATIONAL NEEDS' TELLS US ABOUT CHILDREN?

As we shall see in Chapter 2, giving a child the label 'special educational needs' (SEN) tells us nothing specific enough about a student and his or her learning to begin the conceptualise what might be done to help him or her because the term covers a whole range of areas – learning, behavioural, sensory and so on. In addition, labelling pupils as 'special needs' children, or children 'with SEN', is highly problematic for other reasons.

In schools, as Fulcher (1989) points out, staff may react to children's difficulties in a number of ways. Some might use a frame of reference concerned with what is 'wrong' with children and how this 'problem' can be dealt with. They might be concerned with finding ways of measuring the problem and coming up with a set of planned responses to make them 'better', or as well as possible so that they will 'fit in'. Focusing on what is wrong with a person means emphasizing ways in which she/he is different or deficient, where 'deficiencies' can be 'treated' like an illness. It can often be experienced, especially by the learners themselves, as a very negative way of meeting needs. Where use of the label 'special educational needs' depends on the sense of deficiency in children, it is often seen as reflecting a 'medical' or 'deficit model' of difficulties in learning and/ or behaviour. This model has a sense of being in some way inferior or distant from the norm, for example *dis-, un-, -challenged, difficulty*. This way of looking students' difficulties may in itself prevent a positive approach to diversity and difference.

Other people's frame of reference might be more concerned with children's well-being and their own moral duty to help them. They may worry about the child and feel sympathy for the child's struggles. In some situations, the difficulties that children experience may be seen as a tragedy for the individual and/or the family, and the children were treated like 'charity cases'.

Another frame of reference for understanding difficulties is the social context in which learning takes place. An examination of the physical environment, resources, teaching approaches, the difficulty and/or interest level of the task or activity may show how it can act as a facilitator or barrier to learning. Social factors can turn some differences into disabilities. In a broader context, one might ask, for example, what part economic deprivation and poverty contribute to creating difficulties in learning experienced by children. We might then think about the extent to which 'learning difficulties' might be seen as 'obstacles to learning' arising from the society in which those students live. It might be economic factors, government policy, institutional practices, broader social attitudes or inappropriate physical surroundings that stop people from doing things.

Within school settings, we often see some of these views of the difficulties experienced by children.

CONNOTATIONS OF THE SEN LABEL

Frames of reference associated with the SEN label may carry positive or negative connotations in relation to individual children. On the surface, the notion of fulfilling a 'need' conveys a sense of kindliness. In practice, however, the kind of special or additional provision that is made may imply a value placed on pupils (Salmon, 1998). There may be an assumption of agreement between all the interested parties about what is 'needed' which often (but not always, of course) ignores 'crucial issues' of the lack of power that may be allowed to pupils and parents in the decision-making process. Sometimes, as discussed below, this is associated with a view that interventions should be planned by experts and 'done to' the child with SEN. Cole (2005) reports her own study of the views of teachers who were mothers of children with SEN and notes how the perspectives of the mother-teachers changed when their own children were identified as experiencing difficulties. What they came to value as 'inclusion' emerged as a result of their own individual experiences. They valued the small things that professionals did to make their children and themselves feel included, who tried hard and demonstrated good faith. The specifics of what they wanted for their children in terms of provision differed, but, in the end, they wanted to see their children included in the community. These mother-teachers are reported as taking their role as advocates for their own children and the children with whom they worked very seriously.

Sometimes personal experiences with students can open our eyes to some of the issues related to the labels we give to students.

DISCOURSES AROUND CHALLENGING BEHAVIOUR

11 year old 'Jamie' S was another boy identified as 'having problems', but this time categorised as both disruptive and lazy. He was placed in the 'remedial' band, along with students who experienced difficulty in conceptual development: language, problem-solving, communication and abstract thinking. I taught his group Classical Studies which Jamie loved. He was the first with the answer to everything and was very articulate. At the end of one year, he corrected my version of a tale from Greek mythology that I related many months before. He was right; I was wrong. There was a clear disjunction between the label 'remedial' and my observation of him as articulate, interested and engaged in his learning. He loudly resisted writing tasks because, as I later (but much too late for Jamie) realised, like James above he was dyslexic – and, like James, was educated in a local authority where dyslexia was not recognised. In some lessons he expressed his feelings of frustration with the lack of cognitive challenge and pressure to write with obviously hostile behaviour. In my lessons I was relying largely on narrative so pressure to cope with text did not apply. In the hierarchy of power and influence in schools, those with a professional responsibility for sustaining existing organisational structures may well experience the rejection of school provision by students such as Jamie as challenging to the existing order as well as to themselves. They may then go on to interpret the behaviour of these students, and the students themselves, as deviant and as 'needing' to be cured by a special intervention programme.

(Wearmouth, 2003)

The use of the word 'need' is extremely sensitive in the context of education. 'Need' can be seen as a lack of something in an individual which gives rise to difficulty. A starving person lacks sustenance, for example. 'Need' can also mean the thing the individual requires to satisfy that lack, in this case food and drink. It is not simply the word itself but the issues about who has the power to decide which children have needs, what those needs are and how these should be met (Armstrong, 1994). There is also a question about appropriate expectations of children identified as 'having' SEN. There is a strong relationship between teachers' expectations and student achievement, self-esteem and development that has been well documented since the seminal work of Rosenthal and Jacobson (1968). Salmon (1995) comments on her perception that the term SEN is too often associated with a sense of failure to come up to the mark. Instead of signifying belonging and entitlement, she sees the terms *special* and *need* as 'weasel words' with connotations of helplessness and inadequacy. They are used to justify relegating the problem to a specialist, while at the same time leaving teachers 'feeling helpless and deskilled' (Salmon, 1995, pp. 73–74). In a similar vein, Corbett (1996) comments that students with the SEN label can become marginalised by schools. She asks, 'What does 'special' mean? If we detach this word from its anchor in 'educational' we can see that 'special' does not mean especially good and valued unless we use a phrase like, 'you are a special person'. She notes that 'special' 'is linked to 'needs, implying dependency, inadequacy and unworthiness (ibid., p. 3).

Not all educators take the same view, however. Some, for example Cole (1990), argue that identifying children's 'special educational needs' has a very humanitarian aim. This is to provide additional resources, develop specialist methods to address particular difficulties in learning, or overcome the effects of a disability in order that children can benefit from their education. Without identification of individual needs it is impossible to justify individual attention.

INTERPRETATIONS OF 'NEED'

'Melvin', aged 13, was small, thin, frequently hungry and dirty. He had the reputation of being an incorrigible kleptomaniac. Several times he was found stealing from peers, staff, the local shops and people queuing at the bus stop near the school. Whilst still only 12, he had stolen a local bus and driven it along the high street. He was caught because he was so small that he could only see through the spokes of the steering wheel and passers-by reported a bus travelling along with no driver. Some of his teachers saw him as intrinsically bad and wanted him to be excluded permanently because they thought he was a threat to his peers and to the school. What he 'needed' was expulsion from mainstream and treatment in a special school. The educational psychologist thought he 'needed' hypnotherapy, to 'treat' and 'cure' him. Others took a more charitable view. His problem was not badness within himself, but neglect by his family. They felt that what he really 'needed' was food and clean clothes and that then he would be 'sorted out'.

(Adapted from Wearmouth, 2009)

CONCLUSION

In this Introduction, we have seen how important it is to recognise the frame of reference within which the SEN of children are understood. In my own experience of teaching in eight different schools, it is very clear that this strongly affects how we treat them and the kind of provision that is made.

Chapter 1 below sets the scene for understanding frames of reference commonly used in the area of SEN by discussing a variety of psychological models of human learning and behaviour that have been dominant in educational circles at different times. Chapter 2 then outlines the history of provision for children seen as 'different' from peers on account of learning, physical or behaviour difficulties, and the changes in thinking about such difficulties over time. Chapter 3 focuses on children's difficulties in communication, language and cognition, common indicators of these difficulties, their relationship with learning, and some of the ways that such difficulties might be addressed. Chapter 4 is concerned with understanding and addressing difficulties in cognition and learning, with particular attention given to moderate and specific learning difficulties.

1

MODELS OF HUMAN LEARNING

Behaviourist, constructivist and eco-systemic approaches

INTRODUCTION

Crucial to understanding difficulties in learning and behaviour and ways to address these is familiarity with common frames of reference within which that learning and behaviour is viewed. There is an important, although in some ways simplistic, distinction that we can make between the view that the mind is a passive recipient of knowledge and merely reacts to outside influence and the view that it is proactive in interpreting and constructing the world. In terms of frames of reference from educational psychology, a passive view of the human mind is most commonly reflected in the behaviourist model. Here, all behaviour is assumed to be learned. Underlying behavioural principles is a basic concern with observed events that is what people actually do, not on assumptions about intentions or statements *about* behaviour and its effects. In the world of special needs provision individual education plans have often been drawn up with interventions designed to shape learning and behaviour that are 'done to' the child. The opposite view of the human mind, that it is active in reaching out and constructing meaning, is reflected in frames of reference most commonly associated with constructivist and sociocultural views of learning.

UNDERSTANDING LEARNING FROM A BEHAVIOURIST VIEW

Principles linked to behaviourist psychology (Skinner, 1938; Baer *et al.*, 1968) have often dominated thinking about how to intervene when things are seen to have gone wrong in terms of learning and behaviour in educational institutions (Dwivedi and Gupta, 2000). It is particularly important, therefore, to be familiar with the frame of reference associated with this approach.

UNDERSTANDING PRINCIPLES OF BEHAVIOURISM

Almost all the principles of behaviourist approaches were derived from work with laboratory animals, for example Skinner (1938). Early experiments with animals assumed that all behaviour is learned through a process of conditioning. In a famous sequence of trial-and-error learning tasks, rats learned to press levers in order to find food (Skinner, 1938). Learning involved the formation of a stimulus–response association, that is pressing the lever and finding food, in the rats' memory. Reinforcement through a reinforcer, in this case food, strengthened the association between stimulus and response. If the association between stimulus and response was broken by removing the reward, the rats' behaviour would gradually cease through 'extinction'. The opposite of positive reinforcement is negative reinforcement. Undesirable behaviour is discouraged and desired behaviour encouraged through putting a stop to something unpleasant. Where something unpleasant occurred as a result of an action it is viewed as 'punishment'.

The same behavioural principles have been applied to attempts to modify interactions between teachers and pupils in school contexts. The behavioural model works on the principle that behaviour is learned, and that responses (or behaviours) are strengthened or weakened by their consequences.

When behavioural principles are applied in school settings, the reinforcing conditions or consequences of behaviour as well as the physical and social context in which the behaviour occurs are systematically modified in order to improve students' behaviour. When viewed against the behaviourist frame of reference, behaviour experienced as disturbing is seen as having been learned through positive reinforcement in some way. Most work in response to issues of individual students' behaviour that is perceived as disturbing by teachers has been based 'on behavioural management approaches (which employ strategies such as positive reinforcement, response cost, extinction and so on) where the reinforcing conditions or consequences of a behaviour are adjusted in order to moderate its frequency' (Dwivedi and Gupta, 2000, p. 76). Operant conditioning – reinforcing what teachers want their students to do again, ignoring or punishing what they want students to stop doing – has been widely applied in teaching in UK classrooms since the 1970s (Merrett, 1985). One way to address undesirable behaviour is to identify and alter the stimulus context or setting in which that behaviour occurs. Another way is to ensure that whatever is rewarding and reinforcing is removed so that the behaviour is extinguished. In addition, whenever individuals behave in ways that are seen as more appropriate, they should be rewarded in a way that clearly recognises the greater acceptability of the new behaviour within contexts where that behaviour is clearly acceptable.

In addition to classroom management, behavioural approaches have often been used in the special educational needs (SEN) area for programmed instruction where tasks requiring repetitive practice, like learning multiplication tables, spelling, phonic work and word recognition can be broken down into small stages, and where correct responses by students can be rewarded and reinforced.

APPLYING BEHAVIOURAL PRINCIPLES TO DIFFICULTIES IN BEHAVIOUR AND LEARNING

Behavioural principles can be applied to changing behaviour at individual or group level. W. Rogers (1994a, 1994b), for example, encourages adopting a behavioural approach towards teaching primary school pupils whom he describes as 'behaviourally disordered' to take responsibility for their own behaviour. He notes: 'While most students respond to the normal socialisation into rights-respecting behaviour, some will need to be *specifically taught*'. He goes on to comment, ' … learning targets can be developed as specific *behaviour* plans that involve teacher modelling, student-rehearsal and feedback and encouragement in the natural setting of the classroom' (B. Rogers, 1994, pp. 166–7).

Effective behaviour management is not simply about increasing and decreasing behaviours, but also about teaching students to discriminate between settings (times and places) where certain behaviours are appropriate and acceptable, and other settings where they are not. In Rogers' view, we should not excuse students from 'taking ownership for their disruptive behaviour', 'facing accountability for such behaviour by facing appropriate consequences' or 'learning that behaviour is not an accident of birth or location', and that 'one can learn to make better and more conscious choices about behaviour' (ibid., p. 167).

INDIVIDUAL STUDENT BEHAVIOUR

Individualised behaviour management strategies should make clear to pupils what behaviours are unacceptable and also provide opportunities for modelling, rehearsing and reinforcing behaviours that are acceptable (ibid., pp. 167–9). Behavioural methodology is a scientifically based technology, so the first requirement is a clear definition of the target behaviour. For instance, if a child is thought to be 'hyperactive' Merrett (1985) suggests an operational definition of behaviours such as 'out of seat' will be required. Once the behaviour has been operationally defined, there should be systemic observational sampling across times of day, situations, nature of activity, person in charge and so on. Such observations need to be taken over a period of about 5 days to establish the baseline level of responding. Once the baseline can be clearly seen, an analysis detailing the following three stages should be carried out:

A. the antecedent event(s), that is, whatever starts off or prompts
B. the behaviour, which is followed in turn by
C. the consequence(s).

(Ibid., p. 8)

Merrett advises that when a consequence of a behaviour 'is shown to be maintaining [the] behaviour at a high level then that consequence is, by definition, and regardless of its nature, reinforcing it positively'. Telling children off can temporarily choke off certain behaviours, but these may recur after a very short time. This can be 'very frustrating for the teacher'. However, it may be the teacher's scolding that is maintaining the child's behaviour. 'By definition "ticking off" is positively reinforcing the child's "attention-seeking" behaviour. If that positive reinforcement is removed then the rate of occurrence of the behaviour will be reduced. It will eventually become extinguished' (ibid., p. 9).

Strategies to maximise students' learning of new behaviours include 'shaping' which breaks complex tasks down into a series of steps and ensures that each step is reinforced in a particular sequence. Other procedures include modelling, where students are rewarded for matching the behaviour being displayed for them.

GROUP BEHAVIOUR

One very well-known framework for classroom management that has been based on behavioural principles is that of 'Assertive Discipline' (Canter and Canter, 1992). 'Assertive teachers' communicate expectations to students clearly and confidently, and reinforce words with actions in order to 'manage' students' behaviour in schools. Canter and Canter (1992, p. 12) assert that students need to know 'without doubt' what teachers expect of them, what will happen if they choose not to comply, and that appropriate behaviour will be overtly reorganised. They also need to be taught 'how to choose responsible behavior' (ibid., p. 13).

Canter and Canter (1992, p. 17) see teachers' 'own negative expectations about her [or his] ability to deal with disruptive student behavior' as major factors preventing teachers from asserting themselves in the classroom. Key to successfully manage classroom behaviour, therefore, is teachers' positive expectations of their own ability to do this. Clear rules derived from a behaviourist approach enable teachers to do this. They advocate setting up a classroom discipline plan with three parts: rules, positive recognition and consequences. Rules should be limited in number, focus on observable events, be applicable throughout the time period, apply to behaviour only and may involve students in their compilation. Key to motivating students to choose appropriate behaviour are 'positive reinforcers' which include teacher praise, rewards of various sorts and positive communications with parents. Teachers are exhorted to teach the classroom discipline plan. They are advised to 'explain why you have consequences', to 'teach the consequences' and 'immediately begin reinforcing students who follow the rules'. Rules should be reviewed frequently, at the start of the year and as needed later on. The discipline plan should be posted up in the classroom and sent home to parents (ibid., p. 115).

Canter and Canter recommend that teachers should take the time to 'identify the academic activities, routine procedures and special procedures for which [he or she needs to determine] specific directions' (ibid., p. 123) at the beginning of every year. By 'specific directions' they mean 'identify the classroom situations for which specific directions are needed. Then determine those directions.' Subsequently, 'teach your specific directions immediately prior to the first time the activity takes place.' It is often also helpful to put posters and other illustrations around the classroom 'to help remind students of appropriate behavior during different activities and procedures' (ibid., p. 139).

After implementing the stated consequences of a rule-breaking misdemeanour, teachers should look for every opportunity to recognise appropriate behaviour.

CRITIQUES OF BEHAVIOURAL TECHNIQUES FOR CONTROLLING AND SHAPING BEHAVIOUR

A number of criticisms of behaviourist techniques for controlling and changing behaviour have been commonly expressed. For example, behavioural approaches might serve teachers' wishes to manage students rather than responding to individual needs (Hanko, 1994) and engaging students' interests. These approaches might also lead children into becoming overly dependent on praise. In any case, inappropriate use of praise can be damaging to some students for two reasons. If it not sincere, students may well see through it. Also, students who have learned from previous experiences that they are likely to find learning activities in school difficult will be very discouraged by teachers' obvious lack of understanding of their situation. Consequently, 'a praise-refusing student's determination not to be lured into the risks of failing yet again may be further reinforced' (ibid., p. 166). In every school I taught, I met praise-refusing students who have, seemingly, shut themselves off from teachers. Many have been socially isolated and, to judge by body language, feel appalled at their own loneliness yet cannot do anything about it. I well remember the case of Paul, undernourished, dirty, smelly, and always alone, but hovering as close to the entrance of the school building as he could manage. No amount of attempts by me to 'shape' his behaviour through praise would have enabled him to socialise more with peers.

Behavioural approaches might also encourage students into unthinking conformity to authority (Milgram, 1974). There is an assumption that the school curriculum to which students are expected to comply is appropriate and relevant and that school and teacher processes and practices are equitable and reasonable for all students but we all know that this is not necessarily the case. Further, these approaches tend to ignore the importance of cultural and community contexts, together with the traditional values, in which behaviour is defined and understood (Glynn and Bishop, 1995; Macfarlane, 1997, 2000a, 2000b). There is an assumption that teachers know which types of rewards and sanctions are 'meaningful' to individual students as positive or negative reinforcers. Where teachers do not understand the cultural norms of their students, they may 'mis-cue' in their application of behaviour management strategies. Gee (2000) illustrates this point vividly with an example of a small girl who told a story at the class 'sharing time'. The story was full of rhythm, pattern and repetition and would have been highly valued in the child's family and local community, where oral performance was prized according to its entertainment value. The teacher, however, was anticipating a different (unarticulated) style of oral performance, that of being informative, linear and succinct, and did not appreciate the child's form of storytelling. Subsequently, this child was referred to the school psychologist for telling tall stories.

Sometimes, too, behavioural approaches fail to take adequate account of the emotions. As Hanko (1994) comments,

> emotional factors affect learning, especially if we see only their provocative or withdrawn facade which usually hides children in constant misery, loneliness, self-loathing and fear ... teachers are frequently baffled by children who 'don't respond even to praise', 'spoil their work the moment I praise it', 'just shrug it off' and 'don't seem to care'.
>
> (p. 166)

APPLICATIONS OF A BEHAVIOURIST APPROACH TO NEW LEARNING

Behaviourist principles can be applied when devising programmes for learning new material. A learning sequence using behaviourist principles might be structured by, first, breaking down the new information into a series of small steps, then teaching this information separately and sequentially. The difficulty level of the questions has to be graded so the learner's response is always correct. The learner responds to every question and receives immediate positive feedback and reinforcement of the learning behaviour and the correctness of the response. Good performance in the lesson, in other words the desired behaviour of effort and achievement, is reinforced by verbal praise, prizes and good grades.

Thinking clearly about the next steps in learning can be very useful where a child experiences difficulties in conceptual understanding. Behaviourist approaches to learning in what we might call the basic skills can be very powerful in their effectiveness. Numbers of spelling programmes and basic numeracy programmes using the four rules of number have been devised along these lines, reinforcing the learning through repetitive drill and practise with rewards (reinforcers) for correct responses. However, these approaches cannot apply to all new learning. For example, the requirement for information to be broken down into small steps and for each response to be reinforced immediately restricts what can be learned through this approach. However, not everything can be broken down into a clear sequence of stages that are the same for all learners. There is criticism of these approaches that they can be rigid and mechanical. Although it is useful in learning repetitive tasks like multiplication tables and those word skills that require a great deal of practice, higher order learning is another matter. Further, it is not possible, or desirable, that all new learning should be pre-programmed and that the outcomes should be known in advance because that would deny the importance of, for example, individual critical thinking, personal research and analysis and individual responses to art, drama, music and so on. Also, some educators, for example Hanko (1994), feel that behavioural approaches also fail to address students' ability to reflect on their own learning and achievement adequately.

Even so, behaviourist approaches have been very commonly adopted in schools and can still be identified in many software programmes intended, for example, to encourage awareness of the four rules of number in mathematics, phonics in decoding text and reading and designed to provide immediate feedback and reinforcement of learning.

COGNITIVE–BEHAVIOURAL APPROACHES

Recent years have seen a move away from strict behaviourist approaches toward alternative ways of understanding learning that take greater account of how individuals construct reality for themselves. Cognitive–behavioural approaches have emerged from behavioural psychology and have a number of additional key characteristics, one of which relates to a focus on the way the mind processes information. Cognitive–behavioural approaches can incorporate a wide range of cognitive processes including the use of perception, language, problem solving, memory, decision-making and imagery. For example, in the school situation when students begin to pay attention to 'the stream of automatic thoughts which accompany and guide their behaviour, they can learn to make choices about the appropriateness of these self-statements, and if necessary introduce new thoughts and ideas' (McLeod, 1998, p. 72). This can result in behaviour more appropriate to the school context and lead to a higher level of academic achievement.

TECHNIQUES TO ENCOURAGE METACOGNITIVE AWARENESS OF BEHAVIOUR

In the area of student behaviour in schools, a number of researchers have employed the concept of metacognitive awareness (i.e. awareness of one's own thinking, feelings and emotions) into the area of emotional regulation, or self-management in order to cope with feelings such as violence, bullying, disaffection or isolation (Meichenbaum and Turk, 1976; Shapiro and Cole, 1994). A common application of this approach is to the management of feelings of anger (Harris, 1976; Wilde, 1994, 1995). As Wilde (2001, pp. 192–3) notes, the first step is to encourage students to recognise bodily sensations that precede displays of anger.

One of the simplest ways to teach children to identify their internal body cues is to ask them to respond to the query, 'What do you notice in your body just before you get angry?' Students often reply that they 'feel warm all over', or that they 'notice their pulse is racing', or 'make fists with their hands'. They might clench their teeth, or 'start shaking all over', or 'feel their muscles get tight, especially in their arms'.

(Ibid.)

The intention is to give them the chance 'to distract themselves or walk away before they react' (ibid., p. 192). Distraction involves persuading students to think about something other than the focus of their anger. It can be done through helping them to remember positive events in detail such as the happiest or funniest experience they can remember (ibid., p. 193).

The assumption behind this is that it is almost impossible, for a student to imagine a happy, funny or relaxing scene and still be angry. In another cognitive behavioural approach, De Shazer's (1985) 'solution-focused' narrative continues to be employed in some places. Here, students are invited to work out ways of reaching a positive outcome to particular problems in story form. Students are then encouraged to use their narratives to learn ways of behaving more appropriately in school and/or achieve more highly in academic terms.

CONSTRUCTIVIST APPROACHES

In recent years, there has been an increasing interest in constructivist views of learning with a focus on ways in which individuals actively construct their understanding of the reality in which they live. There is a recognition here that 'the emotional and behavioural difficulties which people experience in their lives are not caused directly by events but by the way they interpret and make sense of these events' (McLeod, 1998, pp. 71–2). How young people think of themselves in school has an enormous impact on their learning and behaviour. Pollard comments that some might be 'highly anxious and continually under-value themselves'. Some can seem 'over-confident and extremely resilient'. Some may know their own strengths and weaknesses while others 'may seem to have relatively naïve views of themselves. Children may be gregarious, or loners, or they may be lonely' (Pollard, 2002, pp. 97–8). Learning is highly dependent on both the context, what the learner makes of the situation in which she/he finds himself and the interaction between them (Greeno, 1998; Lave and Wenger, 1998).

From this view, difficulties in learning and behaviour 'problems' in schools are also situated in the interaction between the context and the perceptions of students (Mehan, 1996; Lave and Wenger, 1998; McDermott, 1999). It is important therefore for adults to understand how children make sense of their own circumstances and what impression is conveyed to students of others' views of them. Adults in schools have to be concerned all the time with the sense that children are making of their worlds, their experiences, tasks in classrooms, and so on. Being open to this demands careful and sensitive listening, observation and reflection. It appears obvious that taking the young person's view seriously is essential to any consideration of how we might reduce obstacles to students' learning (Hart, 1995). Learning programmes are likely to be more effective when students have some sense of ownership over them.

Children, like the rest of us, come to decisions about what learning is worth investing in. They judge whether the benefits of any given learning situation outweigh the time, effort and (in some classrooms) the risk of being wrong and exposing themselves to public humiliation in being thought stupid. Questions of value-to-oneself are at the heart of the learning process. Young people may not make the effort if they do not perceive it as worthwhile in relation to the effort that is required. All learners are active, all learners think about their learning, all have views about it and all have feelings about it, no matter what the context. All learners have some power and control. They may enthusiastically comply with the demands set for them or may outwardly comply but inwardly be resentful. They may be un-cooperative or disruptive and resist the demands made on them. For young people in schools, feeling that they have some control over their learning, understanding why they are learning something, choosing how to do it and when to do it, may be important. Allowing learners some degree of choice in, or power over, what they learn and how they learn invites them to take control over their learning. This is not always easy in busy classrooms. However, offering some choices that can be accommodated within the school day gives learners responsibility and acknowledges that they have preferences, dislikes and ideas.

NOT JUST LITERACY!

Arnold was another student about whom I had many concerns. Over the 2 years I worked with him in a comprehensive upper (13–18) school his written work showed just how little progress he seemed to have made in literacy skills. He just did not seem to care. He came to school in a shirt that was always dirty. He smelled of body odour and nicotine. I never knew what Arnold was thinking. I never knew what he felt about his own lack of literacy. If we had known, it might have made a difference either to our approach or to the outcome educationally. Arnold left school functionally illiterate.

(Adapted from Wearmouth, 2009)

CONSTRUCTING UNDERSTANDING

While Skinner's work was seminal to advances in understanding learning from a behaviourist perspective, a number of researchers have contributed to the way we often think about children's learning from a constructivist view. Two of the foremost theorists are Jean Piaget (1896–1980) and Lev Vygotsky (1896–1934).

JEAN PIAGET

Jean Piaget, a Swiss psychologist, was one of the theorists who contributed a lot to the thinking that children learn by doing. Children's direct experience with their environment is therefore vitally important to their learning. This particular frame of reference made a strong contribution to primary schools organising their classrooms with the children in mind, and providing a rich learning environment with concrete materials and resources. Piaget's research evidence led him to conclude that learners construct knowledge by interacting with their environment and what it is in it and that they re-construct their thoughts in the light of new experiences. As they grow older, learners develop more detailed and accurate understandings or constructions of the things they experience.

LEV VYGOTSKY

Akin to Piaget's model of constructivism but developed in a very different context, that of Soviet Russia, is the social constructivist model of Lev Vygotsky. As Vygotsky suggested, language is also important to the sense-making process in addition to a carefully organised rich learning environment. Vygotsky concluded that it is through interacting with others, especially a more able other, that learning mainly occurs and is developed. This means that relationships among learners themselves and between learners and adults that are bound up with the learning environment are also important.

The next steps in learning of which a child is capable and the range of knowledge and skills that learners are not yet ready to learn on their own but can learn with support from, and in interaction with, more informed and experienced others, for example adults, is called the 'zone of proximal development' or ZPD in this model. Within the zone, the more experienced other is central. Learning involves practice below the zone, for example to encourage the development of skills to automatic level. One important reason why Vygotsky's views have become popular in education circles in recent years is that they give a clear role for the teacher in the person of this more experienced, informed other.

The view of learning just described emphasises the social and cultural context of learning and the role that adults play in supporting that learning, and is often called 'socio-constructivism' (the construction of knowledge in a social context), or referred to as taking a sociocultural perspective on learning. Other leading educationalists, for example Jerome Bruner, have picked up and developed Vygotsky's ideas. The ideas from this view of learning underpin much of the current work on formative assessment – 'assessment for learning' – that is discussed in Chapter 7.

SCAFFOLDING LEARNING

One of the ideas that has been developed from a sociocultural view is that of 'scaffolding' to support learning (Wood et al., 1976). Rogoff (1990) identifies six elements in scaffolding learning. First, engage the learners' interest in the task, and then demonstrate how to do it. Next, if possible, reduce the number of steps needed for the task so learners can recognise their own progress. Then, control frustration and offer feedback so that learners can see their own progress. Finally, find a way to motivate the learners so they continue with the task.

To be successful, the interaction must be collaborative between student and the more knowledgeable other. The scaffolding must operate within the learner's ZPD. The scaffolder must access the learner's current level of understanding and then work at slightly beyond that level, drawing the learner into new areas of learning. The scaffold should be withdrawn in stages as the learner becomes more competent. In schools, the final goal is for the learner to become autonomous, secure enough in the knowledge required to complete the task.

Not all learning requires the physical presence of an adult. Learners need scaffolding from more knowledgeable others, but not too much. Learning is also about participating, for example having the chance to behave as a reader, writer and so on, alongside other readers and writers. Learning is often highly charged with emotion. Feelings accompanying success can be very pleasant and/or exciting. The sense of failure can be very upsetting and/or disturbing, especially when it is a frequent occurrence. Feelings are therefore very powerful in supporting, or preventing learning. Getting the balance right is crucial. This is often especially difficult in school where there is a tendency in most classroom for the adults to talk too much and for the learners to talk too little. Other resources, apart from adults, can scaffold learning also: information technologies, peers, books, materials, pop music and so on.

UNDERSTANDING DIFFICULTIES IN LEARNING

We can only make sense of new ideas and information in terms of what we already know. It is hard to learn unless what we are reading about, listening to or looking at makes sense to us. If we think about reading a novel – or children reading a story book – without a way of a way of relating to the words and the ideas in a passage we are not likely to be interested in it. Children can make sense of new ideas only by relating them to what they already know.

Teachers and other adults in schools are responsible for finding ways to support learners to make connections with what they already know. One straightforward way to do this is to talk with learners of any age about what they do or do not know and encourage them not to be embarrassed to discuss difficulties they might be experiencing. Young people have a right to be heard (Council of Europe, 1966). At the same time listening to what they say is an important part of the process of supporting learning. Misconceptions may be very common and not noticed unless we listen to the learner. Many students in schools experience difficulties in learning in the area of mathematics. 'Karen', aged 14 repeatedly made subtraction errors of the following kind:

$$
\begin{array}{r}
9842 \\
- \ 1357 \\
\hline
8515 \\
\end{array}
$$

She thought that the subtraction rule was always to subtract the smaller from the larger figure, whether the figure appeared in the upper or lower line. She had make the same mistake for years and had never understood why her mathematical attainment was so poor until, one day, she was asked to do a 'think-aloud' in the classroom. The challenge for those with an interest in mathematics education is to understand how to break this pattern. Those teachers who are effective in teaching mathematics to the whole range of student learners are those who take very seriously, and are committed to, developing students' mathematical thinking (Anthony and Walshaw, 2007, p. 1). This commitment is characterised by a number of principles, among which are a recognition that all students can become mathematical learners and a 'commitment to maximise access to mathematics'. Other factors are also important: good mathematical knowledge, student to student and teacher to student relationships, the 'connectedness of both people and ideas', 'interpersonal respect and sensitivity' and 'fairness and consistency'.

Teachers' beliefs, expectations and understandings of all students as active agents in their own learning are as important in the area of mathematics as in any other area of the school curriculum. Effective teachers neither embarrass students nor ignore wrong answers. They use mistakes to enhance the teaching. There is now a large body of evidence that demonstrates the beneficial effects of students being encouraged to articulate their mathematical thinking (Lampert, 1990; O'Connor, 1998; Fraivillig et al., 1999). By expressing their ideas, students provide their teachers with information about what they know and what they need to learn. Hiebert et al. (1997) have found that teacher talk that is effective in supporting mathematical understanding and competence involves drawing out the specific mathematical ideas that students are using to work out the answers to problems, supporting students' understanding of the accepted conventions in mathematics, and sharing other methods and ways of working through mathematical problems.

Effective mathematics teachers often listen to what students have to say and re-frame student talk in mathematically appropriate language. This provides teachers with the chance to highlight connections between mathematical language and conceptual understanding. Many students who experience difficulty in mathematics lack the confidence to speak out in the classroom, however. I well remember the occasion when teaching mathematics to a bottom set of 14-year-old students in a secondary school I was asked by one boy: 'ere, Miss, why do you bother with us when you can teach them clever kids?' As noted already, for students to be prepared to volunteer their answers in mathematics lessons they need to feel safe and know that they will not be humiliated by either the teacher or their peers if they are wrong. The first step for the teacher in all this is probably to ensure this sense of safety for all the students in the classroom.

As a teacher in a secondary school, I frequently noticed a number of pupils who experienced difficulties in literacy acquisition and expression using capital 'b's' and 'd's' in the middle of words, for example 'aBle'; 'saiD'. For a long time I simply corrected these errors. However, after a long time when they persisted I asked the pupils to write the words and talk through what they were doing. They all said that they knew the difference between 'B' and 'D' in upper case, but could not remember them in lower case. When I looked to see how they were writing these letters they made no difference between lower case b's and d's, starting them both at the top and running down to the curve, left or right, at the bottom. It is no wonder that they could not remember the difference. They tried to show that they knew the correct spellings by using upper case that they could clearly distinguish.

What these examples illustrate is how learners try to make sense of a new experience or a new problem by trying to fit them to similar experiences of problems they have met before. If there is a good fit then it is more likely that the learner will understand the current experience or solve the problem correctly. If the gap between the existing knowledge or experience and what is needed to understand the current problem or experience is too large, however, this is unlikely to happen.

Nikki (see above) had gone on making the same subtraction errors because, as she later explained, she was 'useless' at mathematics and was too embarrassed to explain her reasoning. I had simply never thought to ask the boys why they used upper case letters in the middle of words because it did not occur to me that they might have chosen to do this deliberately. Concentrating only on the right answer can mean losing the chance to gain insights into learners' understandings and misunderstandings and, therefore, the opportunities to support learning at the right moment.

AN ECO-SYSTEMIC POSITION

The final frame of reference in relation to learning and behaviour that is taken from psychology and discussed here is the view that the behaviour and learning of individuals can be viewed as part of an ecosystem. The school and the home are seen as being two separate systems with their own individual ways of operating. The eco-systemic approach understands school behaviour and learning problems in terms of dysfunctions in the family system, in the school system or in the family–school relationship system (Campion, 1985; Dowling and Osbourne, 1985). Cooper and Upton (1991), for example, describe the case of 11-year-old John, a student at a special school for students identified as experiencing emotional and behavioural difficulties. At home he reported he was bullied by staff at school, but never complained about this at school. His complaints to his mother meant that she was repeatedly involved in his school life where she acted as his advocate, and elicited protective behaviour from her. Her protection in the school situation was in contrast to the role she played at home where she slept most of the day because she worked in a club at night. 'If the suggestion of bullying by staff was eliminated, it is likely that John would find some other way to elicit positive behaviour towards himself by his mother' (ibid., p. 24). From an eco-systemic approach, there would be an analysis of the system operating in John's home and the roles played by the various members to explain both John's and his mother's repeated behaviours. There would also be an analysis of the roles played by the various members of staff at school in relation to the home situation. An appropriate intervention would need to aim to involve John and his mother in a collaborative relationship usually organised by a consultant family therapist.

> Such consultations may result in the adjustment of systemic structure (Minuchin, 1974), in the form of an adjustment in the roles performed by members of one or other of the systems involved, or in the adjustment of systemic boundaries, whereby weakened boundaries are strengthened, or overstrong boundaries are relaxed.

In the situation of John and his mother, perhaps the home-based relationship between John and his mother was lacking in warmth, 'to the extent that John has to engineer the type of situation described above, in which his mother plays a protective role'. A possible solution for this might be actively to look for a situation where John's mother took a protective role. 'The precise nature of this remedy would be dependent upon the outcome of meetings between the family and the therapist' (Cooper and Upton, 1991, p. 24).

PROBLEM SOLVING SPECIAL NEEDS PROVISION

There is no golden formula for addressing the special learning needs of all students who experience difficulties in schools. There are some general principles, however. Every student is different and every situation is different. Addressing difficulties is a question of problem solving. First, find out about the learner and the difficulties s/he experiences. Then think about the requirements of the particular curriculum area and barriers to learning in the classroom environment and in the particular curriculum area. Finally, reflect on and implement what will best address those barriers to help the learner achieve in the classroom.

CONCLUSION

How we understand learning and what lies at the root of a 'learning difficulty' in school has a very strong influence on how we respond. Over the years, different social or psychological understandings have given rise to different interventions.

Recent research confirms that strategies recommended for particular SEN are useful for most students. Lewis and Norwich (2000) point out that there is little evidence that staff should use entirely different teaching approaches for most students with SEN. Instead they suggest that staff should give students more time to solve problems, more chances to practise their skills, more examples to learn from and more experience of using knowledge and skills in different situations. They should also provide more strategies to help learn information and skills, more preparation for the next stage of their learning, and more frequent assessment of what is and what is not being learned and why

The extent to which children qualify under the legal definition as children 'with special educational needs' depends to a large extent on the policies and resources within their Local Authorities and educational settings as well as the wording of particular Education Acts. In the next chapter, we will look at teachers' current legal responsibilities in teaching children identified as having SEN, set against the context of a historical perspective on special education.

SPECIAL EDUCATIONAL NEEDS

Evolution of the field

INTRODUCTION

In Chapter 1 we saw how our own experiences and values as human beings and professional educators influence the way in which we interpret difficulties experienced by students in schools (Fulcher, 1989; Wearmouth, 2009). Chapter 2 begins with an overview of the history of provision for children seen as 'different' from peers on account of the learning or physical difficulties they experienced, or the behaviour they displayed, and continues with a discussion of the way that schools' thinking about learning, behaviour and children's rights has changed over time.

DEVELOPMENT OF THE 'SPECIAL' EDUCATION SECTOR FOR THE FEW: A HISTORICAL PERSPECTIVE

The way in which educational provision is currently organised is a product both of its own history and of the values, beliefs and political ideology of our society (Wearmouth, 2009). Over the years, special education provision has been characterised by a number of recurring themes. For example, there is the question of whether to separate off children who experience difficulties of various kinds into special segregated provision, or integrate them into mainstream. Then there is an issue of what kind of curriculum should be offered: whether it should be the same for all children, or different for some groups. Echoing down the years, for instance, has been discussion around the academic-vocational/manual divide. There has also been discussion about whether, and how, to classify children into the various groupings of difficulties. As a corollary of this, if classification is seen as appropriate, what characterises the differences both between the groupings themselves and between the children so classified and others? How children in the various groups should be and/or are valued, and the value that can be deduced from the kind of provision that is deemed to be appropriate is also important. For many years, too, there was debate about whether some young people are capable of being educated in any form that is recognisable as 'education' at all.

Other ongoing discussion and debate includes the question about why the special education sector was developed in the first place. Were special education systems created by caring professionals wishing to address the needs of children in difficulty more effectively? Is special education provision essentially benevolent? Did it evolve primarily to help children who were different in some way, or experienced difficulties? Did special educational provision develop to serve the economic and commercial interests of society? Did these interests dictate that as many people as possible with difficulties should be productive and contribute to an industrial society? Certainly businessmen 'played a part in the founding of pioneer establishments for the deaf and for the blind, and that throughout the nineteenth century trade training took up much of the lives of the handicapped attending them' (Cole, 1990, p. 101). Did it, perhaps, develop to provide a means to exclude troublesome pupils, or pupils who required a lot of the teacher's time, from mainstream classes? For example, when a new national system of secondary schools was designed in the 1944 Education Act, did the smooth running of those schools demand the exclusion of some pupils, for example those categorised as 'educationally subnormal'? Are there vested interests from, for example, the medical profession and psychologists, that support the existence of special provision?

SPECIAL EDUCATION PROVISION: THE EARLY YEARS

As Warnock (1978, ch 2) notes, early institutions for children who experienced difficulties of various sorts were founded by individuals or by charities, rather than government agencies, and catered only for a few. Later, central government intervened, initially to support and supplement what was provided through voluntary agencies. Later still the government created a national framework for special education provision, but it was not until the 1970s that this framework included the entitlement of all children to an appropriate education.

The early institutions were very different from today's schools. They were designed to focus on moral improvement, training in work skills, and the Christian religion (Oliphant, 2006) often for adults as well as children. In Britain they began in the second half of the eighteenth century, first with schools for blind and deaf children. For instance, the School of Instruction for the Indigent Blind, established in 1791 in Liverpool, together with other private foundations that quickly followed it, including the School for the Indigent Blind in London founded in 1800 and the Asylum and School for the Indigent Blind at Norwich in 1805, were solely concerned in instructing inmates in the Christian faith and in earning their living. They relied on adult and child labour to make a profit in their workshops. The inmates were obliged to spend several hours a day praying or listening to readings from the scriptures as they worked. Oliphant (2006, p. 55) notes that the School of Industry in Liverpool was, according to its founding plan, intended, along with religion

> to furnish the blind with employment that may prevent them from being burdens to their family and community.... The Plan required that 'habits of industry' be formed with men making baskets, tablecloths and whips while the women spun yarn, made sail-cloths and picked oakum.

As recipients of public charity, the inmates had little freedom of choice and this, together with a focus solely on religion and work could provoke misdemeanours. As the Liverpool School Visitors' Books records, those who missed Sunday service or fell asleep in church might be punished through the use of a 'bread and water table'. There were also instances of 'miscreants being locked in the beer cellar for a week for offences such as refusing either to be washed or to wear shoes instead of clogs'. In 1825, two boys were flogged for insolence and another for 'making away with his yarns' (Oliphant, 2006, p. 58). It was not until other schools were founded thirty years later that educational aspects were introduced into the curriculum, for example in the London Society for Teaching the Blind to Read in 1838.

Only a small proportion of blind children went to school. Most blind children's prospects were 'pretty grim' (Cobham, Foreward to Bell, 1967, p. 11) and there were very few attempts to challenge the general attitude to the educability of the blind. One of the most significant, however, was the foundation of the 'College for the Blind Sons of Gentlemen' in 1866 in Worcester. Bell (1967, p. 16) notes that its aims, as published in its 1872 report, were 'to bestow a sound and liberal education upon persons of the male sex afflicted with total or partial blindness, and belonging by birth or kinship to upper, the professional or the middle classes of society'. (The equivalent for girls was not established until 1921, by the National Institute for the Blind (NIB) in Chorleywood.) Academic goals were very high and set towards the professions of the Church, Law and Education. Football, cricket, swimming and athletics were merged with the academic side of the curriculum. Foster, headmaster of the College, felt: 'If prosecuted steadily, systematic physical exercises will greatly diminish ... that ungracefulness of bearing which has helped to confirm the impression of the blind man's inferiority' (Bell, 1967, p. 22). Worcester College remained the only route for blind children to achieve higher qualifications and entry into the professions until after the Second World War, however.

The first schools for the deaf were also very limited in the education they offered. The first was founded in Edinburgh in the 1760s: Mr Braidwood's Academy for the Deaf and Dumb. It took in a small number of paying pupils who were taught to speak and read. As Warnock (1978, p. 9) comments, although the education they provided was subordinated to training, 'many of their inmates failed to find employment on leaving and had recourse to begging'.

Attempts were made to teach a trade to girls with physical disabilities from poor homes in the Cripples Home and Industrial School for Girls established in Marylebone in 1851, and to boys in the Training Home for Crippled Boys founded in Kensington in 1865. Again, the children were expected to work for their living and produce goods for sale.

For those children who experienced serious difficulties in learning, until the end of the nineteenth century there was little provision apart from workhouses and infirmaries for those who needed secure care. The first specific provision made for them was the Asylum for Idiots established at Highgate in 1847 which took people of all ages. By 1870 there were five asylums. Only three professed to offer any kind of education. For children to be admitted to these institutions parents had to agree to them being certified as 'idiots', a label that attracted much odium (Cole, 1989, p. 22).

School boards were established under the terms of the (1870) Forster Education Act in England and Wales, and the (1872) Education (Scotland) Act, and charged with ensuring provision of elementary education in places where there were insufficient places through voluntary enterprise. They did not specifically include disabled children, but a few school boards did admit blind and deaf children to ordinary elementary schools or to centres attached to these schools.

EDUCATION FOR (ALMOST) ALL

These Education Acts established the foundations of elementary education. However, not all areas took it up. The government became increasingly involved and after 1880 attendance was made compulsory for most children until the age of 13. Large numbers of children came to school for the first time. Many appeared to have poor intellectual ability and made little or no progress. Up till now those children who experienced less serious learning difficulties had largely managed with day-to-day living in a society that was a lot less complex than ours. However, now that they were compelled to attend school their presence was felt to be holding others back in the large classes that existed in public elementary schools. The question was what to do with them especially as national level funding for individual schools and, therefore, teachers' salaries, depended in part on the outcomes of examinations of pupils conducted by school inspectors as, for example, in England between 1963 and 1890 when the policy was abandoned. Cole (1989, p. 40) outlines evidence presented to the Sharpe Report (Education Department, 1898) of what might happen to these children. 'In London, before 1892, the feeble-minded over 11-year-olds had been mixed with 5-year-olds in Standard 1.' However, teachers were 'so concerned with getting their average children through the Standards and so conscious of HMI's [inspectors'] expectations that they would send the feeble-minded to play in a corner with a slate'.

In 1889, a Royal Commission distinguished between three groups of children seen as experiencing varying degrees of learning difficulties: 'feeble-minded', 'imbeciles' and 'idiots'. Feeble-minded should be educated in 'auxiliary' schools away from other children, imbeciles should be sent to institutions where education should concentrate on sensory and physical development and improved speech. 'Idiots' were not thought to be educable. These days we would consider the use of these labels for children unacceptable. However, in the nineteenth century there was a big difference in status and respect given to those groups of students who had been identified as 'different' from the rest. The Sharpe Report comments that, by 1897, 27 special schools had been founded in London for 'feeble-minded' children. Even at that time, however, there were parents who felt that there was a stigma attached to their child's placement in a special class, and resisted it. One witness to the Sharpe Committee said that parents 'will admit anything except that their children are defective in intellect' (Cole, 1989, p. 40).

The same Royal Commission recommended compulsory education for the blind from age 5 to 16, and for the deaf from age 7 to 16. Deaf children, generally considered slower to learn on account of difficulties in communication, were to be taught separately by teachers who should be specially qualified to do so.[1] Legislation in Scotland followed in 1890 with the Education of the Blind and Deaf Mute Children (Scotland) Act, and in England and Wales in 1898 with the Elementary Education (Blind and Deaf Children) Act. It was not until 1938 when the (1937) Education (Deaf Children) Act came into effect that deaf children were compelled to attend school aged 5.

In 1896, a Committee on Defective and Epileptic Children appointed to investigate the need for special provision for some pupils recommended that school authorities should make provision for all 'defective' children in their area and be able to make attendance compulsory. This included children with physical disabilities. However, special provision is expensive, and the 1899 Elementary Education (Defective and Epileptic Children) Act merely gave permission for school boards to make such provision.

In 1902, the old school boards were abolished and a two-tier system of local education authorities (LEAs) for elementary and secondary education was established. County and county borough councils were given powers to provide secondary education for blind, deaf, defective and epileptic children. The Mental Deficiency Act of 1913 required LEAs in England and Wales to ascertain and certify which children aged 7 to 16 in their area were defective. Those judged by the authority to be incapable of being taught in special schools were to pass to the care of local mental deficiency committees.

Two further Acts compelled authorities to provide for the education of 'mentally defective' children and physically defective and epileptic children: the Elementary Education (Defective and Epileptic) Act (1914); and the Education Act (1918) respectively. However, the (1929) Wood Committee Report concluded that only one-third of those children who were 'mentally defective' under the terms of the 1914 Act had actually been assessed and, of these, only one-half were attending special schools.

In Scotland, the Education of Defective Children (Scotland) Act of 1906 empowered school boards to make provision in special schools or classes for the education of defective children between the ages of 5 and 16, while the Mental Deficiency (Scotland) Act of 1913 required school boards to identify children in their area who were 'defective'. Those children who were considered ineducable became the responsibility of parish councils for placement in an institution.

In 1921, an Education Act consolidated previous legislation, requiring children in the four categories of blind, deaf, mentally and physically defective (but not 'idiots' or 'imbeciles') and epileptic to be educated. 'Defective' and epileptic children should be certified by LEAs and then educated in special provision of which there was a whole range made by both voluntary bodies and LEAs. As Warnock (1978) comments, the statutory foundation of special provision continued broadly until the 1944 Act. Blindness and deafness were not defined and there was no provision for the identification and certification of these children. The parents of children in any of the four categories were required to see that their child attended a suitable special school from the age of 5 in the case of blind or deaf children, or 7 for other children, until the age of 16. LEAs had the duty to ensure the provision of such schools.

THE RISE AND DEMISE OF OPEN-AIR SCHOOLS FOR DELICATE CHILDREN

To understand the current form and organisation of special educational provision we have to be aware of the social, political and ideological context from which that provision derives (Wearmouth, 2009). The rise and demise of a particular form of special provision that no longer exists serves to illustrate this point: open-air schools for 'delicate' children.

The foundation of open-air schools in Britain at the beginning of the twentieth century has to be seen against a context of concern that had arisen around the physical well-being of large numbers of children, particularly in the cities where the air was often heavily polluted and living conditions for most people were wretched. As Cole 1989 notes, recruitment of soldiers to fight in the Boer War had highlighted the large proportion who were medically unfit to fight. As a result of this concern the government passed the Education (Provision of School Meals) Act in 1906 to enable LEAs to provide school lunches and, in 1907, the Education (Administrative Provisions) Act to require LEAs to carry out medical checks on all their pupils. Gamlin (1935) notes how open-air schools were modelled on a German example. In the Berlin Education Authority a school doctor examining children observed that many of them were anaemic and debilitated. He strongly recommended open-air treatment, suitable surroundings, careful supervision, good feeding, and exercise and, as a result, the first open-air school was established in 1904 in pine woods in Charlottenburg. The first British open-air school was Bostall Woods, founded in Woolwich, in 1907. This was soon followed by others in which 'pupils with weak hearts, bronchial complaints or suffering from malnutrition were subjected to a somewhat Spartan regime' Lessons were 'spent out of doors or in three-sided rooms, with meals provided and a compulsory rest period in the middle of the day' (Cole, 1989, p. 51).

Classrooms in Aspen House open-air school in Streatham, London, had floors and roofs but no walls and were completely open to the elements. When it rained, children on the end of the rows might get wet. In winter, if it had snowed, the children might have to clear it off the tables and chairs before they could start the lesson. There was no heating but, however cold it became, lessons continued and pupils just had their clothes and blankets with which to keep warm. A medical official in Leicester noted that, among the characteristics of children admitted to these schools were 'Stunted growth, loss of muscular tone and dryness of hair [and] rings around the eyes, long silky eyelashes, inflammation of the eyelids, enlarged glands, anaemia, feeble circulation and shallow breathing' (Cathcart, 2005). Thousands of children in Britain matched this description, particularly in city slum areas. This, combined with the cheapness of schools that were effectively three-sided sheds with corrugated iron roofs, led to an expansion of their numbers. By the 1930s there were 4000 children a year from London who were sent to open-air boarding schools. They might be funded by LEAs, charities or private philanthropists, for example, the Cadbury family in Birmingham.

The Independent newspaper (23 January 2005) carried interviews with some of the ex-pupils of such schools. George Cooke, 84, recalled the cold of a 1930s winter at Brent Knoll School, south London. As a 10-year-old he wore shorts like all other boys at the time and was given a blanket to keep warm. Others remembered more positive aspects of open-air schools. Norman Collier, aged 82, considered he and other children benefited academically. He, for example, became a company director later on in life. Frances Wilmot, an asthmatic who was a pupil at Uffculme in the 1950s, remembered small classes and caring teachers, a great contrast with some of the children's own homes.

Doubts about the value of open-air schools had crept in as early as 1930 when a report from the Industrial Research Board questioned the value of being out of doors in all weathers. These doubts were increased when medical officers surveying open-air schools for the Ministry of Education in 1949–1950 commented:

> When the canvas curtains were drawn, rain drove in and above the curtains so that the floor and furniture were often wet. We saw children scraping frozen snow off the desks and chairs before they could be used.
>
> (Cole, 1989, p. 113)

Even so, in 1955 12,000 'delicate' children were still being educated in open-air schools in England and Wales. However, medical opinion was moving away from favouring Spartan conditions for 'delicate' children. In addition, improved standards of living, slum clearances, the advent of the National Health Service, the arrival of antibiotics, notably streptomycin that reduced the incidence of tuberculosis and the provision of milk and meals in schools meant that the open-air movement gradually became redundant.

DEVELOPMENTS IN DIFFERENTIATED CURRICULA FOR DIFFERENT LEARNERS

Towards the end of the Second World War, a coalition government reorganised the education system through the 1944 Education Act in England and Wales and sought to develop a common national framework for the education of a diverse student population. The creators of the 1944 Act formalised a system of selection based on the results of assessment techniques that, they believed, could differentiate different 'types' of learners. They thought it possible to design different curricula for different learning 'types' who could be educated in separate sectors of the system. In mainstream, students took an examination at the age of 11 and were selected into different types of secondary school: grammar, technical and secondary modern. Within individual mainstream schools students were selected into ability 'streams'. Students might be directed into academic or work-related programmes according to measured 'ability'. It seemed to many that the educational hierarchy that developed was fair. Students appeared to be able to rise to a level which reflected their ability. Also, it was based on psychometric testing which at that time was thought by many educators to be reliable and valid.

In the area of special education, the 1944 Education Act, Sections 33 and 34, set out the legal basis for subsequent provision. The duty of LEAs to ascertain which children required special educational treatment, hitherto confined to defective and epileptic children, was extended to children with all types of disability, generally described in the Act as 'pupils who suffer from any disability of mind or body'. These days we might call this way of viewing difficulties in learning as the 'medical' or 'deficit model'. Certification of defective children within the education system was abolished. Any child considered educable would have access to schooling. Children seen as ineducable in school were to be reported to the local authority for the purposes of the Mental Deficiency Act 1913. Local authorities were empowered to require parents to submit their children for medical examination. In Scotland, the Education (Scotland) Act 1945 repeated much of the content of the Education Act 1944.

The Handicapped Students and School Health Service Regulations 1945 in England and Wales developed a new framework of eleven categories of students: blind, partially sighted, deaf, partially deaf, delicate, diabetic, educationally subnormal, epileptic, maladjusted, physically handicapped and those with speech defects. Maladjustment and speech defects were included for the first time. The College of Speech Therapists was founded in 1945. Between 1949–1954, the number of speech therapists employed by LEAs increased from 205 to 341 and the number of children treated annually rose from 25,098 to 44,800. The regulations required blind, deaf, epileptic, physically handicapped and aphasic children to be educated in special schools. Children with other disabilities could attend mainstream if there was adequate provision (Warnock, 1978, p. 2.46).

Official guidance in 1946 estimated that the number of children who might be expected to require special educational treatment, not necessarily in special schools would range between 14–17 per cent of the school population.

During the years which followed, the two groups which continually expanded in numbers were those students considered 'educationally sub-normal' (ESN) and those identified as 'maladjusted' (Warnock, 1978).

> The category of educationally subnormal children was seen as consisting of children of limited ability and children retarded by 'other conditions' such as irregular attendance, ill-health, lack of continuity in their education or unsatisfactory school conditions. These children would be those who for any reason were retarded by more than 20% for their age and who were not so low-graded as to be ineducable or to be detrimental to the education of other children. They would amount to approximately 10% of the school population. Detailed suggestions were made for provision. In large urban areas about 1–2% of the school population would need to be educated in special schools (including 0.2% in boarding schools); the remaining 8–9% of the school population would be provided for in ordinary schools.
>
> (Warnock, 1978, p. 2.48)

The number of children in ESN special schools nearly doubled between 1947 and 1955 from 12,060 to 22,639. Even so, the number of children awaiting placement was over 12,000. Politicians increasingly looked to medicine and the growing profession of psychology for solutions to behaviour in schools that was construed as deviant (Ford, 1982). Warnock (1978) notes that education authorities in Scotland were empowered in 1945 to provide a child guidance service which would advise teachers and parents on appropriate methods of education and training for these children. By 1966, 25 of the 35 education authorities had a child guidance service. In England, the number of child guidance clinics increased from 162 in 1950 to 367 20 years later. To keep pace with this kind of expansion in numbers, the Summerfield Working Party (1968) recommended new and expanded arrangements for training of educational psychologists and a doubling of numbers. In 1978, an Her Majesty's Inspectorate (HMI) survey of behavioural units found that 239 special units for disruptive children had been established in 69 of the 96 LEAs in England.

The Education (Handicapped Children) Act 1970 removed the power of health authorities to provide training for children who experienced the most serious difficulties in learning (deemed 'mentally handicapped') and required the staff and buildings of junior training centres to be transferred to the education service. Around 32,000 children in institutions of various sorts together with an unknown number at home now became entitled to special education. In future they were to be regarded as 'severely educationally sub-normal' (ESN(S)), as opposed to the moderately educationally sub-normal (ESN(M)) group who had previously made up the ESN category. In Scotland the 1974 Act also gave education authorities responsibility for the education of children who previously had been viewed as 'ineducable and untrainable'.

EDUCATION FOR ALL

The system established after 1944 and intended to make appropriate provision for the whole pupil population of the nation seemed stable. However, as Clark et al. (1997) note, many commentators in education began to see that the system of selection into grammar, technical and secondary modern schools was not as fair as was first thought. For example, differing proportions of students were selected for each type of school in different areas of the country. Considerable doubt was increasingly thrown on the reliability and validity of the psychometric tests that were used to discriminate between children, and there was obvious overlap between the learning needs of students in mainstream and special schools (Wearmouth, 1986). In addition, movement between school types was very difficult indeed, regardless of the amount of progress made by individual students. Further, a growing concern for equality of opportunity in society at large led some researchers in education to comment that the system was divisive and functioned to sustain the position of some already advantaged societal groups. For example, Douglas (1964) and Hargreaves (1967) found a disproportionate number of middle-class children in grammar schools.

The result of all this was, beginning in the 1960s and increasingly in the 1970s, the establishment of comprehensive schools, the introduction of special classes and 'remedial' provision in mainstream, and the integration of some children from special to mainstream schools.

INTRODUCTION OF THE CONCEPT OF SPECIAL EDUCATIONAL NEEDS

In 1978 a review of special educational provision in Great Britain for children and young people was published in the Warnock Report. It introduced a new concept of 'special educational needs' (SEN) to replace previous categorisation 'by disabilities of body or mind'. Following Warnock teachers were advised to plan on the assumption that one in five children would have 'special educational needs' at some time in their school career. Official guidance in 1946 estimated that the number of children requiring special educational treatment might be up to 17 per cent of the school population. A study by Rutter *et al.* (1970) had enquired into the incidence of difficulties in learning in the school population. The report from this study showed teachers' perceptions that, on average, 20 per cent of their students were experiencing difficulty of some kind. Since that time, the figure of 20 per cent has been used to estimate the number of children nationally who might experience difficulties. Of the total number of students, approximately 2 per cent are seen by policy makers as likely to have difficulties which require additional or extra resources to be provided. This figure of 2 per cent is clearly useful to resource-providers, for example LEAs, to estimate what proportion of their resources they are likely to have to set aside for individual students' educational needs. However, it is an arbitrary one, drawn from a count of students in special schools in 1944 (Warnock, 1978). The law, focusing as it does on individual need, gives no such figures for the incidence of children likely to need statutory assessment. However, LEAs, whose duty it is to implement legislation, have used such Department for Education and Employment (DfEE) guidance to establish general criteria for assessment.

The 1981 Education Act attempted to translate the Warnock Report into legislation. The 11 categories of handicap were replaced with the view that pupils' difficulties occur on a continuum, and that a 'special educational need' exists if a child has 'significantly greater difficulty in learning' than peers, or a disability that hinders him or her from using educational facilities normally available in the local school.

Local authorities were given responsibilities to identify needs which called for provision in addition to that normally available in the school. Parents should be consulted about provision for their child, and could appeal against a local authority's decisions. All children should be educated in mainstream schools but with certain provisos: that their needs should be met there, and that it was compatible with the education of other children and with the 'efficient use of resources'.

DIFFERENCES IN VIEWS

Locally and nationally different pressure groups pursue a wide variety of conflicting goals. For instance, many people within the Deaf community feel that it is vital to their culture that their children go to their own schools. They want them to be allowed to learn within a signing environment which draws upon a rich heritage and sense of self-identity. Some organisations, such as Barnados and Scope, run their own schools. In many local authorities, too, it is possible to find campaigns run by schools and parents to keep special schools open. Equally, organisations such as the Centre for Studies on Inclusive Education (CSIE), Parents for Inclusion, and the Alliance for Inclusion work hard to promote the closure of special school provision and the development of mainstream schools that are open to all. Similarly it is possible to find individual parents and children involved in comparable battles. The press and Internet are full of stories of people fighting to get their child into (or back into) a mainstream setting or fighting for them to be removed from mainstream and placed in a special school.

INCLUSIVE OR SPECIAL SCHOOLS?

The tension between including children with difficulties and segregating them into special provision has surfaced repeatedly. 'In every age, many concerned professionals have been reluctant to segregate the handicapped' (Cole, 1990, p. 106). The Sharpe Report of 1898, for example, contains a report from Dr James Kerr of the Bradford Schools Board that teachers wished 'to get rid of these [so-called feeble-minded] children' so that they would have fewer problems in schools and classrooms (Education Department, 1898, p. 19). However, another contributor to the report stated that opinion was divided on the subject. However, 'there appears to be amongst the teachers … a general agreement that the children, where they are tractable, are as well, if not better, in the ordinary schools under ordinary arrangements' (Education Department, 1898, p. 216). In this Report, teachers were reported as wanting 'to exclude only the openly disruptive children and the severely handicapped' (Cole, 1990, p. 102).

Decisions about whether inclusive mainstream, or special schools, are more likely to meet children's learning needs are not always clear cut. Two groups of students about whom teachers often express very serious concerns are those whose experience profound and complex difficulties in learning who may also have acute physical disabilities, and those whose behaviour is perceived as very threatening and disruptive. It may be that some students are so vulnerable that the overriding consideration for them is a protective environment where their individual care needs can be considered together with their education. Whether the actual location is a mainstream or special site may be of less relevance than other considerations. The quality of the specialist facilities to support children's physical requirements, the level of understanding between students and staff and the effectiveness of the system of communication between home and school are very important irrespective of location. In relation to the second, the proviso that students 'with special educational needs' should be educated in mainstream schools provided that this is compatible with the education of peers is often seen as the justification for placement in an alternative location.

In 1997, the government issued a Green Paper 'Excellence for All Children' to which over 3000 parents/carers responded. The ratio of parental responses favouring special as opposed to mainstream provision for students who have Statements of Special Educational Needs was 20:1. The sample of parents responding cannot be considered a cross section of those who children have a Statement. Mostly these Statements referred to educational needs arising from sensory impairments or multiple and complex difficulties in learning. One of the reasons given for supporting special provision was that physically disabled children were often perceived to suffer at the hands of non-disabled peers. 'Children can be treated like, and feel like, a freak if they are integrated as individual disabled children' (letter from parent). One parent wrote: 'The worry caused when your child is being bullied or feeling depressed affects the whole family. Taking an Asperger child out of that environment greatly increases the quality of the child's life as well as the family'. There was also a view that, although the same opportunities are often not available to students in special schools as those in mainstream, this does not mean these opportunities automatically become available if the child is moved into mainstream. These opportunities must be made available within the special schools rather than transferring the children to mainstream. In addition, there was a perception of intolerance by children and staff in mainstream, of gross dissatisfaction with levels of resourcing, staff training, awareness and understanding in mainstream, and a perception that special schools constitute a 'reservoir of shared knowledge and expertise in teaching' of students with specialist needs. The minority of parents wanting a mainstream education for their children had equally strong views on their children's rights to be respected as full members of society. In preparation for this they felt it most appropriate that they should be included in local mainstream schools with additional provision to meet their individual needs.

The Ofsted (2010). review in England found that no one model – such as special schools, full inclusion in mainstream settings, or specialist units co-located with mainstream settings – worked better than any other. The effective practice seen during the review encompassed a wide range of models of provision, often with significant flexibility in the way in which services were provided within any one local area. However, it became apparent during the review that the pattern of local services had often developed in an *ad hoc* way, based on what had been done in the past rather than from a strategic overview of what was needed locally.

The key implication of these findings is that any further changes to the system should focus not on tightening the processes of pre-scribing entitlement to services but, rather, on improving the quality of assessment and ensuring that where additional support is pro-vided, it is effective. Ofsted felt that it was important to improve teaching and pastoral support early on so that additional provision is not needed later and develop specialist provision and services strate-gically so that they are available to maintained and independent schools, academies and colleges. Legislation should be simplified so that the system is clearer for parents, schools and other education and training providers, ensuring that schools do not identify pupils as having SEN when they simply need better teaching. Those pro-viding services for children should focus on the outcomes for the children and young people concerned.

LEARNING DIFFICULTIES, DISABILITIES AND THE LAW

In England and Wales, the aspect of law currently relating to SEN is Part IV of the 1996 Education Act (Part 11 of the Education Order 1996 in Northern Ireland). Under the terms of this Act a child 'has *special educational needs* if he or she has a *learning difficulty* which calls for *special educational provision* to be made for him or her'. That is, a child only has 'special educational needs' when special provision is required to meet them: learning difficulties do not in themselves constitute such a need.

In understanding the legal definition of SEN fully, we need to understand what is meant by 'learning difficulty'. In the parts of the UK governed by Education Acts passed by parliament in London, a child has a learning difficulty if:

a. he has a significantly greater difficulty in learning than the major-ity of children of his age,

b. he has a disability which either prevents or hinders him from making use of educational facilities of a kind generally provided for children of his age in schools within the area of the local edu-cation authority.

(Education Act 1996, S. 312, http://www.legislation. gov.uk/ukpga/1996/56/contents; DENI, 1998, para. 1.4)

In law, a learning difficulty creates a need. The need is 'special' if the provision required to satisfy it is 'special'. A student might have a 'learning difficulty', for example, if she/he has a specific literacy difficulty which makes it hard to engage in the same learning activities as other students. This much is fairly obvious – but a child might also have a 'learning difficulty' if she/he has a physical disability that creates a barrier to moving around the school or classroom to participate in those activities with peers.

This way of defining a learning difficulty raises a number of questions. Included in them are how to measure 'significantly greater difficulty in learning' and how to compare one student to the majority. Comparing individuals against what we feel most people at that age should be learning and the way they should be learning it is bound to lead to mistakes, leaving some children without support and others with support that is unnecessary. Then there is a question of how to gauge the contexts in which a difficulty becomes significant, for example whether remembering names is difficult only in examinations, or in everyday learning situations also. Finally, what is meant by a general level of provision? Some schools have space for particular sporting activities, others do not, for example. All teaching staff tend to adapt their classrooms to suit their way of working.

The majority of those who might be defined as having learning difficulties will experience difficulties of a mild nature. Whether they are identified as needing additional support is very variable in different parts of the country. It is not unusual for schools to use formal curriculum attainment levels as a general marker in an attempt to identify children with learning difficulties or disabilities. In England, for example, practitioners will often identify someone as having learning difficulties if they are working two or more National Curriculum levels below the majority of their age group. The danger here is that this allows assessment designed for a different purpose to validate decisions which affect provision and children's learning. Inevitably, whatever system is used to define students' needs, the professional, resource and policy judgments involved in the decision-making process will always leave room for inequality.

The second part of the definition in the 1996 Education Act refers to a 'disability' as causing learning difficulties. This means that, by law, a person with a visual impairment has a learning difficulty if the individual cannot access the same facilities as peers. This aspect of the definition of learning difficulty means that, if LEAs and schools provide appropriate learning opportunities, then no child would be hindered 'from making use of educational facilities generally provided' (Education Act 1996, S. 312; DENI, 1998, para. 1.4), and therefore no child would have SEN.

SPECIAL EDUCATIONAL NEEDS AND DISABILITY ACT 2001

Another piece of legislation may well affect the teaching role in schools. This is the Special Educational Needs and Disability Act (SENDA) 2001. In 1981 the law said that all children should attend mainstream schools, provided three conditions were met. First the child must receive the special provision that he or she requires. Next, the child's placement must be compatible with the 'efficient education' of other children in the same school. Finally, the child's placement must be compatible with efficient use of available resources.

Although there was a legal duty to include children in mainstream schools, these three conditions meant that some LEAs could argue that some children should go to special schools, even against their parents' wishes. This law has now been changed to increase children's rights to be educated in mainstream. A child who has SEN and a statement of SEN must now be educated in mainstream school with two conditions: the wishes of the child's parents and the provision of efficient education of other children.

Stronger rights to a place in a mainstream school, have made it unlawful for schools and LEAs to discriminate against disabled students, particularly in relation to admission arrangements and the educational provision in school. The SENDA gives parents (not children) the right of appeal to the Special Educational Needs and Disability Tribunal, if they feel their child has suffered discrimination. Parents have a right to say where they want their child to go to school. However, they do not have the right to insist on their own choice of school.

THE DISABILITY DISCRIMINATION ACT 2005

A further piece of legislation, the Disability Discrimination Act (DDA) 2005 is pertinent to the work of teachers in classrooms. In this Act the definition of disability in Section 1 says a disabled person has a physical or mental disability which has an effect on their ability to carry out normal day-to-day activities. The effect must be substantial (i.e. more than a minor or trivial) AND adverse AND long term (has lasted or is likely to last at least a year or for the rest of the life or the person affected).

The DDA stresses planned approaches to eliminating discrimination and improving access and is nationwide (including private education), imposing duties on schools and local authorities. It places a duty on public bodies to promote disability equality.

Disability Equality Duty (DED) legislation came into force in December 2006, requiring all public bodies, including schools, to be proactive in promoting disability equality and eliminating discrimination. The duty required schools to plan, develop and evaluate the impact of provision and to involve disabled pupils, disabled staff, families and other users of the school in doing so (adapted from http://nationalstrategies.standards.dcsf.gov.uk/node/249402, accessed 28 March 2011).

The Equality Act passed into law on 6 April 2010 with many of its provisions coming into effect in October 2010. The intention of the Act is to consolidate previous discrimination legislation.

RESPONDING TO INDIVIDUAL NEEDS

When a teacher is seriously concerned about the progress made by a child in a classroom, it is very important to be aware of the process that should be followed to maintain the child's access to education.

THE CODE OF PRACTICE

In 1994, the government published a *Code of Practice for the identification and assessment of special educational needs* (DfE, 1994) for use in England and Wales. The Code was designed to offer 'statutory guidance' to schools in England and Wales to address issues of how to provide appropriate support to those with learning difficulties. A similar publication was produced later in Northern Ireland (DENI, 1998). In Scotland the legal framework and associated advisory documents are different.

In 2001, a revised *Special Educational Needs Code of Practice* (DfES, 2001; National Assembly of Wales, 2004) was implemented, offering statutory guidance to LEAs, governing bodies and schools.

The guidance suggests that children's learning needs may fall generally into one of four areas.

Children will have their needs and requirements which may fall into at least one of four areas. Many children will have inter-related needs. The impact of these combinations on the child's ability to function, learn and succeed should be taken into account. The areas of need are:

- communication and interaction
- cognition and learning
- behaviour, emotional and social development
- sensory and/or physical.

(DfES, 2001, p. 74)

A list of the sorts of support appropriate to each area is outlined in the Code. We will return to this in later chapters.

The Code of Practice makes the assumption that teachers will offer differentiated learning opportunities, and that 'the culture, practice, management and deployment of resources in a school or setting are designed to ensure all children's needs are met' (DfES, 2001, para. 1:6, p. 2). If however a child fails to make adequate progress then additional or different action should be taken.

Adequate progress can be defined in a number of ways. It might, for instance, be progress which:

- closes the attainment gap between the child and their peers;
- is similar to that of peers starting from the same attainment baseline, but less than that of the majority of peers;
- matches or betters the child's previous rate of progress;
- ensures access to the full curriculum;
- demonstrates an improvement in self-help, social or personal skills;
- demonstrates improvements in the child's behaviour;
- prevents the attainment gap growing wider.

(DfES, 2001, para. 4.14)

The 2001 Code of Practice recommends a graduated approach to individualised interventions through provision at 'School Action' or 'School Action Plus'. 'School Action' begins when a class teacher, SEN coordinator the Special Educational Needs Co-ordinator (SENCO) or teaching assistant identifies a child as having SEN that require individual provision additional to, or different from, a differentiated curriculum and strategies that are usually provided in the class. The school receives no additional funding for the child. 'School Action' is likely to involve consultation between the class teacher, the school's SENCO and the parents, collation of information already available about the child's progress, and closer attention to the child's programme of work in the classroom, and closer monitoring of progress.

School Action Plus is for children who are likely to need support from specialists outside the school, often a teacher from the special needs support service of a Local Authority (LA), and an educational psychologist. Others might include therapists of various kinds: speech, physio- and/or occupational, health professionals: nurses, health visitors, doctors, education welfare officers and social workers, member of the local child guidance or family guidance team, and specialist teachers for children with physical or visual disabilities or hearing impairments.

School Action and School Action Plus are the responsibility of the school. Class teachers should know which children have been identified at School Action and School Action Plus, contribute information about children's progress at each stage and be aware of the content of children's Individual Education Plans (IEPs). They are also expected to take a leading role in monitoring and recording of children's progress and work with the school's SENCO and with professionals from outside the school.

After the stage of School Action Plus a request for a statutory assessment might be made. If so, the process is handled by the school and the LA, and may result in a Statement of Special Educational Needs that outlines special educational provision determined by the LA.

STATUTORY ASSESSMENT OF SEN

Of the children that schools identify as having SEN, a small proportion are the subject of a Statement of Special Educational Need. According to Ofsted (2010), about 1.7 million school-age children in England, that is, just over one in five pupils, are identified as experiencing SEN. Since 2003, in England the proportion of pupils identified as needing additional support in school at School Action or School Action Plus has increased from 14.0 per cent to 18.2 per cent in 2010, while the proportion of pupils with a statement of SEN has slightly decreased from 3 per cent to 2.7 per cent.

A Statement is a legal document. Provisions specified on it are mandatory. Children with such statements tend to be those who have longer term or more severe disabilities or difficulties. They are usually made the subject of a Statement of Special Educational Need for one of two reasons. Either they need guaranteed access to special resources and expertise, a special curriculum, or an environment with higher than normal staff support. Or their parents, or the professionals responsible for them, want them to attend a special school, or some other form of special provision such as a resource base in a mainstream school.

By law a Statement has to describe the child's SEN, and the special educational provision required to meet those needs. This must include the objectives of the requisite provision, the resourcing, how progress will be monitored, the name of the school, and any 'non-educational' needs and provision that have been identified. These might include services to meet medical needs.

The special provision listed must be provided by law, and the school named must admit the child. Chapter 7, the 'Statutory Assessment of Special Educational Needs' in the 2001 *Code of Practice* outlines the assessment and identification process that is required. The LA has to involve parents at many points, and parents have a number of legal rights. The LA must also collect evidence and advice from several professionals, including the child's head teacher, a doctor and an educational psychologist.

LOCAL AND REGIONAL DIFFERENCES

Around the United Kingdom the different practices and policies of LEAs (Library Boards, in Northern Ireland) as well as issues of ethnicity and socio-economic factors associated with the family, age and gender have resulted in very different levels and kinds of provision for students:

- in 2000 students in Wales were nearly twice as likely to have statements of SEN as in the numbers of students with "Records of Need" (the equivalent of statements) in Scotland
- throughout the UK girls receive less SEN support

- middle-class children are more likely than working-class children to receive the label of dyslexia
- African Caribbean students are far more likely than their white peers to be labelled as having Emotional, Behavioural and Social Difficulties (EBSD).

(Open University, 2005, p. 8)

There is enormous variation in the development of policy and funding priorities. Some LAs ration provision and define Special Educational Needs according to available resources, some support inclusive schools on the one hand, others special schools and Pupil Referral Units (PRUs). There is no consistency across the United Kingdom and no requirement from government for consistency. In 2001, for example, in Manchester, a disabled student was more than seven times as likely to be placed in a segregated special school than a child in the London Borough of Newham, which has actively pursued a policy of inclusion since 1985 (DfES, 2002).

The Ofsted (2010) review of SEN reported that, for some young people, the current system works well and supports clear educational progress. Schools and outside agencies collaborated effectively to serve the child's best interests rather than their own priorities. What seemed to make the difference was rigorous monitoring of children's progress, speedy intervention and thorough evaluation of the impact, together with high expectations for the child and a determination to support young people's self-direction. However, this does not seem to be the norm. The outlook for pupils currently identified as having SEN overall is not particularly positive. Ofsted (2010) reports that, as a group, they are disproportionately from disadvantaged backgrounds, they are more likely to be absent from school or to experience periods of exclusion, and their academic achievement and progress at any specific age is comparatively poorer than their peers. These outcomes have not changed very much over the past 5 years. Once they have past the age of compulsory education, young people who experience difficulties in learning or disabilities comprise one of the groups most likely to be unemployed and/or not to be in education.

Consistency in the identification of SEN varies widely, between and within different local areas. Between the three children's services, education, health and social care, there are widely different thresholds for qualifying for additional support. Access to a range of appropriate provision for children with the most severe needs is relatively quick, however, and start at an early age. Identification of need and entitlement to additional provision for young people between 16 and 19, varies across education providers.

Ofsted (2010) reports that the young people interviewed during their review of SEN identified that what they wanted for their future was the same as other young people might wish for: successful friendships and relationships, personal choice about who to live with and what to do in their leisure time and the opportunity of employment. Parents and families often felt that current provision for their children was not supporting them to attain their goals. Identification of their children's needs and fair access to high-quality services to meet those needs was inconsistent. Some felt that the system forced them to 'fight for the rights' of their children, and that the only way to guarantee additional support was through a Statement.

THE SPECIAL EDUCATIONAL NEEDS CO-ORDINATOR (SENCO)

The role of SENCO developed in response to the Education Act of 1981. In the Code of Practice the responsibilities are defined as:

In preschool settings (DfES, 2001, para. 4.15)	In primary and secondary schools (DfES, 2001, paras. 5.32 and 6.35)
• ensuring liaison with parents and other professionals in respect of children with SEN • advising and supporting other practitioners in the setting • ensuring the appropriate IEPs are in place • ensuring that relevant background information about individual children with SEN is collected, recorded and updated	• overseeing the day to day operation of the school's SEN policy • co-ordinating provision for students with SEN • liaising with and advising fellow teachers • managing the SEN team of teachers and learning support assistants • overseeing the records on all students with SEN • contributing to the in-service training of staff • liasing with parents of children with SEN • liasing with external agencies including the LEAs support and educational psychology services, health and social service and voluntary bodies

The role of the SENCO has developed considerably since the publication of the (2001) Code. It may be allocated to members of the school senior management team or class teachers. SENCOs may have responsibilities both at the level of the individual children and the whole school. They may take charge of budgeting, resource allocation, time-tabling and other managerial and administrative roles. They may also work with individual students, as well as advising, appraising and training staff, and liaising with outside agencies, professionals and parents.

Cole (2005) notes how school ethos of the school and the values of individual head teachers have a direct impact on the role, status and, therefore, power of the SENCO to work towards an inclusive culture in the school. Without the support of the senior management team SENCOs can face a very heavy workload with vulnerable children who are not particularly popular in schools in competition with each other for position on league tables of pupil outcomes.

INDIVIDUAL EDUCATION PLANS (IEPs)

Current legislation and guidance refers to an IEP for recording the nature of a student's difficulties and how they are going to be addressed. It is expected that both parents and students will be actively involved in creating and assessing the effectiveness of the IEP. The plan might include adaptations to normal classroom activities, or a special programme of individual work for the child, or both. It should also include criteria for judging success, a section for recording outcomes and a date for reviewing the plan. The student's progress can then be reviewed regularly to see if the aims of the IEP are being achieved.

A number of criticisms have been levelled at IEPs. They can be too bureaucratic. They may include targets for the child which can be demotivating if focused only on weaknesses that the student should attempt to overcome. Sometimes targets are written by teachers or teaching assistants (TAs) without any consultation with the individual learner and may not be appropriate or intelligible to the student. They may focus only on the student and not take account of factors in the learning environment that may be contributing to his or her difficulties.

However, IEPs can also be used very effectively in the process of analysing needs and planning the next steps in a learning programme. This process should be negotiated between all of those working with a student as well as the student him/herself so that it will be meaningful and have a direct impact on ways of thinking and working.

These days some SENCOs have dispensed with IEPs for some children and use group plans instead. Some may rely on 'provision maps' which can be either documents that identify provision for individual children, or whole-school provision with analyses of student outcomes and value for money, or both.

CURRENT DEFINITIONS: THE FOUR AREAS OF 'NEED'

The 2001 Code of Practice (DfES, 2001, para. 7:52) recommends that formal assessment and subsequent provision should address four 'areas of need' described as:

1. Communication and interaction

The range of difficulties will encompass students and young people with speech and language delay, impairments and disorders, specific learning difficulties, such as dyslexia and dyspraxia, hearing impairment and those who demonstrate features within the autistic spectrum; they may also apply to some children and young people with moderate, severe or profound learning difficulties. The range of need will include those for whom language and communication difficulties are the result of permanent sensory or physical impairment.

(Ibid., para. 7:55)

2. Cognition and learning

Children who demonstrate features of moderate, severe or profound learning difficulties or specific learning difficulties, such as dyslexia or dyspraxia, require specific programmes to aid progress in cognition and learning. Such requirements may also apply to some extent to children with physical and sensory impairments and those on the autistic spectrum. Some of these children may have associated sensory, physical and behavioural difficulties that compound their need.

(Ibid., para. 7:58)

3. Behaviour, emotional and social development

Children and young people who demonstrate features of emotional and behavioural difficulties, who are withdrawn or isolated, disruptive and disturbing, hyperactive and lack concentration; those with immature social skills; and those presenting challenging behaviours arising from other complex special needs, may require help or counselling ...

(Ibid., para. 7:60)

4. Sensory and/or physical needs

There is a wide spectrum of sensory, multi-sensory and physical difficulties. The sensory range extends from profound and permanent deafness or visual impairment through to lesser levels of loss, which may
only be temporary. Physical impairments may arise from physical, neurological or metabolic causes that only require appropriate access to
educational facilities and equipment; others may lead to more complex
learning and social needs; a few children will have multi-sensory difficulties some with associated physical difficulties. For some children
the inability to take part fully in school life causes significant emotional
stress or physical fatigue.

(Ibid., para. 7:62)

Clearly there is a lot of overlap between these areas. For example,
in terms of communication and interaction, lack of facility with
receptive and expressive language has important implications for
cognition and learning. A number of teaching approaches seen as
appropriate for addressing the learning needs of students who experience difficulties either in communication and interaction or in
cognition and learning common to both areas:

- flexible teaching arrangements;
- help in/with ... language;
- help ... in acquiring literacy skills;
- help in organising ... help with organisational skills.

(Ibid., paras. 7:56 and 7:58)

Teachers and schools are expected to implement the National
Curriculum inclusion statement (DfEE/QCA, 1999). This sets out
three principles: setting suitable learning challenges, responding to
students' diverse learning needs and overcoming potential barriers
to learning and assessment for individuals and groups of students.

Inclusive teaching in this context means adjusting learning objectives to suit individual students' needs. Not every student is expected
to be working on the same learning objectives as every other student
in the class. It also means teaching that draws on a variety of
approaches, for example open and closed tasks, short and long tasks,
visual, auditory or kinaesthetic activities. It implies, too, understanding that the learning context itself can support, or hinder, learning.

For example, science laboratories with high benches and stools, or art rooms with little rooms between tables, chairs and easels may be very difficult for students with restricted movement. The acoustic environment is important for the attainment of all students, but particularly for those who experience auditory difficulties.

Some students who experience difficulties in learning can work on the same learning objectives as others in the class, as long as the teacher plans appropriate access strategies. For example, a teacher might build in alternatives to written recording, and/or provision of appropriate age and culturally related resources. Disability legislation, as described in this chapter, calls modifications to learning and teaching programmes 'reasonable adjustments'. For example, if a barrier to a mathematics lesson on problem solving is a dyslexic student's lack of fluent knowledge of number facts, she/he may need to use a calculator. If, however, the barrier is a motor co-ordination difficulty that prevents accurate drawing of shapes and graphs, she/he may need the use of appropriate software which is programmed to draw shapes and graphs. If it is difficulty with use of abstract symbols she/he may benefit from the use of concrete materials of some kind. Teachers need to try out ideas and assess results to develop their own practice. Strategies that do not result in improved learning and/or behaviour can be seen as experiments leading teachers towards solutions, not failures.

CREATING A POSITIVE LEARNING ENVIRONMENT FOR ALL

Recent research confirms that strategies recommended for particular SEN are useful for most other students (Lewis and Norwich, 2000). It might therefore be sensible for newly qualified teachers to concentrate at first on strategies which improve the learning environment and increase the range of teaching strategies rather than assuming that something different has to be organised for every individual.

SUMMARY

Over the years, the conceptualisations of differences between people, the development of notions of entitlements and human rights, and the change in focus of, and on, education itself, have all contributed to the complexity and changing nature of the field of SEN.

The term 'special educational needs', used since Warnock (1978), is part of the discourse which, according to Salmon and Corbett, for example, suggests a deficit model. At the same time we must recognise, along with the Disability Movement, that failing to acknowledge difference can be counterproductive to the learning needs of a student and be interpreted as disrespectful to that person's life experiences. Whatever an individual's view, parents, teachers and other professionals in education have to conform to aspects of the official definitions when engaged on formal processes under the Act such as assessment and statementing.

NOTE

1 It is interesting to note that teachers in special schools for children with visual and auditory impairments still require specialist qualifications but those in some other kinds of special educational institutions do not.

3

UNDERSTANDING AND ADDRESSING DIFFICULTIES IN COMMUNICATION AND INTERACTION

INTRODUCTION

The chapter will focus on the first of the four broad areas of need outlined in the *Code of Practice for Special Educational Needs* (DfES, 2001): communication and interaction.

The overlap between communication and interaction, and cognition and learning, will be highlighted. Particular attention will be given to speech and language delay, autistic spectrum disorders (ASD), moderate to severe learning difficulties exemplified by Down's syndrome, and profound and multiple learning disabilities, to illustrate:

- what is known about these delays and disorders from rigorous, high-quality research studies,
- the relationship between such delay, impairment and/or disorder and learning,
- ways by which the difficulties experienced by young people can be addressed through attention to the learning environment, curriculum and teaching approaches.

Issues related to permanent sensory impairment will be discussed in Chapter 6.

COMMUNICATION, LANGUAGE AND COGNITION

Communication is vital in everyday life. It allows us to build and sustain relationships, to share experiences, to express our thoughts and feelings and understand those of others and to learn. As the National Deaf Children's Society (2010, p. 8) states, there is a close link between language and communication. However, they are not synonymous. Language is 'the words (vocabulary), phrases, grammar and expressions we use and how we organise them to communicate'. Language ability can be seen as both receptive (i.e. comprehending what is said and/or written) or expressive (i.e. putting thoughts coherently into words, verbal or written). During their first year of life babies usually acquire a lot of receptive language. By the age of one, children can often understand quite a lot of what is said. However, they are less able to express themselves verbally. 'Communication is really more the means by which we convey language, both to get our meaning across and to understand the meaning of others' (ibid.). Communication is crucial for social and emotional development. It involves not only language, but also 'other things like eye contact, gesture, tone of voice, facial expressions and body language'.

STUDENTS WITH LANGUAGE IMPAIRMENT

Difficulties in language acquisition may involve receptive or expressive language impairments. The first of these is less obvious than the second and can create barriers to learning if overlooked. It is really important for teachers to get to know their students very well and to check carefully that what has been said is properly understood.

PRAGMATIC LANGUAGE IMPAIRMENT (FORMERLY 'SEMANTIC–PRAGMATIC' DISORDER)

Children identified as having a pragmatic language impairment (PLI), previously called 'semantic–pragmatic' disorder, can provide great challenges in the classroom (Smedley, 1990; Adams and Lloyd, 2007).

Many children experience significant difficulties in understanding language and developing vocabulary (Bishop and Adams, 1989; Botting and Conti-Ramsden, 1999). Children who have PLI have difficulties developing conversational skills, such as turn taking and adhering to the topic of the conversation (Bishop, 2000). Some are insensitive to their listeners and talk endlessly about their own preoccupations and interests. Some experience problems understanding discourse and telling stories in a logical order (Norbury and Bishop, 2003); and have problems with over-literal use of language, and making and understanding inferences (Leinonen and Letts, 1997). Some children are competent in using the formal structure of language while experiencing difficulties in semantic understanding (Rapin and Allen, 1983). There are no accurate figures for children who experience these difficulties (Law *et al.*, 2002). Teachers and speech and language therapists report that there are increasing numbers of these children, although Rutter (2005) suggests that the increased numbers may relate to better identification rather than a real increase in prevalence.

Adams and Lloyd's (2007, pp. 229–30) description of a successful classroom intervention illustrates how both immediate and hidden meanings of language and communication, as well as the pragmatics of grammatical structure, have to be made explicit to some children. Their intervention had three principal aspects. First good practice 'in interacting at an appropriate social and language level with the child' was established. The language demands in the classroom were modified, typically by 'having an assistant translate language into short meaningful utterances' accompanied by a visual demonstration. Then the children were taught 'the vocabulary of social situations and insight' into others' emotions. Changes to routines were added in small steps, and these were discussed before they were implemented. Children were supported to understand 'social and verbal inferences, metaphors and hidden meaning in language'. Finally, work on the pragmatics of language focused on 'explicit exercises and classroom support in exchange structure, turn-taking, topic management, conversational skills, building sequences, cohesion and coherence in narrative and discourse'. The teaching methods that were used included 'modelling and individual practice; role-play; practising specific pragmatic skills in conversations; ... promoting self-monitoring and coping strategies ...'.

THE EXAMPLE OF 'AUTISM'

In 1934, Leo Kanner (1943) identified a difficulty in a small group of young children that seemed to centre around excessive focus on the self. He called it 'early infantile autism' from the Greek αυτος (autos) meaning 'self'. This difficulty was marked by inability to relate to people and social situations from early life marked by profound 'aloneness', failure to use language fluently to communicate and anxious and obsessive desire to maintain sameness. It was also characterised by fascination for objects which are handled with skill in fine motor movements, a good rote memory, over-sensitivity to stimuli and apparently good cognitive potential.

Reflecting on his own experience of being autistic, Sinclair (1993) commented,

> Autism isn't something a person has, or a 'shell' that a person is trapped inside ... Autism is a way of being. It is pervasive. It colours every experience, every sensation, perception, thought, emotion and encounter, every aspect of existence. It is not possible to separate the autism from the person – and if it were possible, the person you'd have left would not be the same person you started with.
>
> (http://www.autreat.com/dont_mourn.html)

Around the same time as Kanner, Hans Asperger in 1944 used the term 'autistic' to denote a range of traits in some ways similar to that commented on by Kanner. As Wing (1996) notes, this range included extreme egocentricity and an inability to relate to others, speech and language peculiarities, repetitive routines, motor clumsiness, narrow interests and non-verbal communication problems. Asperger identified features additional to those already seen by Kanner. These were, first, sensory sensitivities and unusual responses to some sensory experiences: auditory, visual, olfactory (smell), taste and touch. In her recollections, Grandin (1996) described her hearing as like a microphone in a hearing aid, permanently at the full volume position. She saw herself as having two choices, either to turn the microphone off altogether, or turn it on and be swamped with sound. Another account of autism (Barron, 1992) includes a description of a boy's super sensitivity to the texture of food and needing to touch and feel it before it went into his mouth. Food had to be of one kind; for example bread could not be made into sandwiches with fillings otherwise it provoked vomiting.

Asperger also noticed an uneven developmental profile, a good rote memory and circumscribed special interests, and motor coordination difficulties. He noted, too, that one in ten people with ASD have what appear to be extremely well-developed skills in one specific area. These skills are often found in areas such as music, art, mathematical calculations and calendrical calculation.

Wing and Gould (1979) identified a 'triad of impairments' in a broader group of 'autistic' children, about 15 in 10,000. This triad covers difficulty in social interaction (difficulty with social relationships, e.g. appearing aloof and indifferent to other people), social communication, both verbal and non-verbal, and imagination. In addition to this triad, repetitive behaviour patterns are a notable feature, as well as a resistance to change in routine.

While the groups share the same triad, there is some difference in emphasis. People with Asperger Syndrome are often 'of average, or above average, intelligence' (National Autistic Society, 2004). There are some social communication difficulties and delay in language development is not likely. In autism, however, three quarters of the population have difficulties in learning, some at a severe level.

Each area within the triad implies particular barriers to learning. Impaired social understanding and relating clearly affect interactions with other children and adults. A child who lacks social understanding is unlikely to understand unwritten social rules, recognise other's feelings or seek comfort from others. Grandin (1996) recalls pulling away when others tried to give her a hug because being touched overstimulated her senses and overwhelmed her. Autistic children may appear to behave 'strangely' or inappropriately, and may often prefer to be alone. Grandin remembers always wanting to participate in activities with other children but not knowing how and never fitting in. She tried to work out how to behave from observing other people and learning through trial and error. Difficulties in social communication mean that people on the autistic spectrum often find it hard to understand the meaning of gestures, facial expressions or tone of voice. Difficulties with social imagination mean people with ASD are unable to think and behave flexibly. This may result in restricted, obsessional or repetitive activities and difficulties in developing the skills of playing with others. Children often find it hard to understand and interpret other people's thoughts, feelings and actions, predict what will or could happen next and understand the concept of danger. They may also find it hard to engage in imaginative play, prepare for change and plan for the future and cope in new or unfamiliar situations.

All is not insurmountable, however. Dumortier (2004) comments from his experience that many of his problems could be avoided by prior planning. Schedules were very important to him and he needed to know well in advance what was going to happen, how it would happen, who would be involved and so on. Any change of plan, including either being late or being early, could lead to feelings of frustration, powerlessness, anger and anxiety.

SPECIALIST APPROACHES TO ADDRESSING AUTISM

Typically, autism in young people is identified through agreed diagnostic criteria consisting of a profile of symptoms and characteristics of autistic behaviour. According to the National Autistic Society in the United Kingdom (2004), the exact causes of autism are still not known, although there is evidence that genetic factors are implicated. Research also indicates that a variety of conditions affecting brain development which occur before, at or soon after birth are associated with autism. What is needed in educational terms to support the learning of students with severe forms of autism is a 'specialist' approach and 'structured support' (http://www.autism.org.uk/about-autism/autism-and-asperger-syndrome-an-introduction.aspx).

Nind (1999) makes the point that much of the literature on autism emphasises an innate inability to learn from natural interactive processes (Jordan and Powell, 1995; Trevarthen *et al.*, 1998). Many of the approaches for children with autism, for example Daily Life Therapy (Higashi), Treatment and Education of Autistic and related Communication Handicapped Children (TEACCH) and Lovaas (Jordan *et al.*, 1998) rely on training or teacher direction, and less on intuitive responding. In the current climate, the prevalent position is that individuals with autism need direct training and behavioural intervention (Nind, 1999).

Daily Life Therapy is intended as a holistic approach to education through the three 'fundamental pillars' of vigorous physical exercise, emotional stability and intellectual stimulation. Young people are taught to 'use vigorous physical exercise to learn to regulate their biological rhythms of life' in order to develop 'awareness of one's surroundings, and concentration that result'. The approach is 'highly structured' and uses 'group dynamics' in order that teachers can 'bond closely with each student to achieve emotional stability so that understanding and trust can develop through "heart to heart" education' (http://www.bostonhigashi.org/about.php?id=8, accessed 29 November 2010).

The TEACCH (1998) is what might be described as a 'cultural' approach to addressing difficulties related to autism. Cultivating individual strengths and interests is combined with structured teaching. TEACCH's approach is that it does not look 'simply for environmental stimuli that might trigger particular behaviours'. Instead it considers the way the child 'reads' their environment. 'TEACHH considers the environment in terms of how the child will be able to interact and learn from it ... a TEACHH-influenced classroom places a large emphasis on physically structuring the room to facilitate learning interactions' (Sheehy, 2004, p. 347).

The Lovaas approach, on the other hand, is a form of applied behaviour analysis (ABA) which is built on behavioural methods such as reducing identified tasks into small discrete 'teachable' steps reinforcing appropriate behaviours associated with each step, and using highly structured intensive teaching strategies. (See Chapter 5 for discussion of ABA.) ABA is used to reduce stereotypical autistic behaviours such as repetitive body movement through 'extinction' and the learning of socially acceptable alternatives to such behaviours.

GENERAL CLASSROOM APPROACHES TO ADDRESSING AUTISM

In classrooms teachers can address the learning and behavioural needs of children on the autistic spectrum in a number of ways. For example, a teacher can pay close attention to clarity and order, reduce extraneous and unnecessary material in order that children know where their attention needs to be directed and maintain a predictable physical environment with very predictable and regular routines, ensuring that everything is kept in the same place. Children might be taught agreed signals to be quiet or to call for attention. Teachers might provide specific low-arousal work areas free from visual distractions. Headphones might be made available to reduce sound. They might also provide a visual timetable with clear symbols to represent the various activities for the day, and a simple visual timer with, for example, an arrow that is moved across a simple timeline to show how much time has passed and how much is left.

The future quality of life for young people with ASD may well depend on how far they can learn to understand and interact with others rather than solely on the academic skills and qualifications they may have gained (Jordan and Powell, 1995). In order to develop greater understanding of personal emotions children might be taught in a very deliberate, overt and structured way to name their feelings and relate these to their own experiences, predict how they are likely to feel at particular times and in particular circumstances, and recognise the signs of extreme emotions such as anger. A visual gauge showing graduated degrees of anger in different shades of colour can often be helpful here.

Pupils might also be taught, again very deliberately and in small steps, to identify and name others' feelings and link these to possible causes, and identify appropriate responses to others' emotions. They might, for example, keep a feelings diary in which they record times when they feel happy, sad or frightened, and what they can do about this. Teachers might use art, drama and social stories to identify the different kinds of emotions and/or explore their physical aspects and/or talk through situations that need to be resolved. Above all it is really important to get to know the pupil really well and to understand his/her individuality, strengths, weakness, likes and dislikes and so on.

CONDITIONS ASSOCIATED WITH MODERATE TO SEVERE LEARNING DIFFICULTIES: THE EXAMPLE OF DOWN'S SYNDROME

There are a number of conditions often associated with some impairment of cognitive ability. One of these is Down's syndrome. Children with Down's syndrome tend to have a lower-than-average cognitive ability, often ranging from mild to moderate difficulties in learning. A small number have severe to profound mental disability. The average IQ of children with Down's syndrome is around 50 (Dykens and Kasari, 1997), compared to the average IQ of 100.

Language skills show a difference between understanding speech and expressing speech, and commonly individuals with Down's syndrome have a speech delay (Bird and Thomas, 2002). Fine motor skills are delayed and often lag behind gross motor skills and can interfere with cognitive development. Effects of the disorder on the development of gross motor skills are quite variable. Some children will begin walking at around 2 years of age, while others will not walk until age 4. Physiotherapy, and/or participation in other specially adapted programmes of physical education may promote enhanced development of gross motor skills.

A 'syndrome' is a group of recognisable characteristics occurring together. Down's syndrome (Down syndrome in the United States and some other countries) was first described in detail by an English doctor, John Langdon Down, in 1866. It is a congenital condition which randomly affects about 1 in 1000 babies born throughout the world, male and female alike. A 'congenital' syndrome is the one present at birth.

Down's can occur in any family of any race, culture, religion or socio-economic class. It occurs because each of the body's cells contains an extra copy of chromosome 21. It can be identified in a foetus with amniocentesis during pregnancy, or in a baby at birth. It is chromosomal, not caused by anything the parents may have done before or during pregnancy.

In the United Kingdom, around one baby in every thousand is born with Down's syndrome, although it is statistically much more common in babies with older mothers. At maternal age 20–24, the probability is one in 1562; at age 35–39 the probability is one in 214 and above age 45 the probability is one in 19 (Huether et al., 1998). There is also data to suggest that paternal age, especially beyond 42 also increases the risk of a child with Down's syndrome (Fisch et al., 2003).

PHYSICAL CHARACTERISTICS

Down's syndrome is recognisable at birth because of the typical physical characteristics (Selikowitz, 2008). Common physical features include a small chin, round face, protruding or oversized tongue, almond shape of the eyes, shorter limbs, a single instead of a double crease across one or both palms, poor muscle tone and a larger than normal space between the big and second toes. The medical consequences of the extra genetic material are highly variable and may affect the function of any organ system or bodily process.

Health concerns for individuals with Down's include a higher risk of congenital heart defects, recurrent ear infections, obstructive sleep apnoea and thyroid dysfunctions (Selikowitz, 2008). The incidence of congenital heart disease in children with Down's syndrome is up to 50 per cent (Freeman *et al.*, 1998). Eye disorders are relatively common. For example, almost half have strabismus, in which the two eyes do not move in tandem (Yurdakul *et al.*, 2006). In the past, prior to current treatment, there was also a high incidence of hearing loss in children with Down's syndrome. These days, however, with more systematic diagnosis and treatment of ear disease, such as 'glue ear' (see Chapter 6) almost all children have normal hearing levels.

When some of the cells in the body are normal and other cells have trisomy 21, it is called mosaic. There is considerable variability in the fraction of trisomy 21, both as a whole and among tissues.

COGNITIVE DEVELOPMENT

Overall cognitive development in children with Down's syndrome is quite variable. It is not currently possible at birth to predict the capabilities of any individual reliably, nor is the number or appearance of physical features predictive of future ability. Since children with Down's syndrome have a wide range of abilities, and success at school can vary greatly, which underlines the importance of evaluating children individually (Selikowitz, 2008).

Individuals with Down's syndrome differ considerably in their language and communication skills. It is common for receptive language skills to exceed expressive skills. Augmentative and alternative communication (AAC) methods, such as pointing, body language, objects or graphics are often used to aid communication.

ISSUES OF HUMAN RIGHTS

Some of the ways in which children with Down's syndrome were portrayed in the past and the treatment that some received illustrate a number of the issues related to human rights and values discussed already in this book. For example, owing to his perception that children with Down's syndrome shared physical facial similarities such as folds in the upper eyelids (epicanthal folds) with those of the Mongolian race as identified by the German physiologist and anthropologist, Johann Friedrich Blumenbach, John Langdon Down used the term *mongoloid*. He wrote in 1866:

> A very large number of congenital idiots are typical Mongols. So marked is this, that when placed side by side, it is difficult to believe that the specimens compared are not children of the same parents. The number of idiots who arrange themselves around the Mongolian type is so great, and they present such a close resemblance to one another in mental power, that I shall describe an idiot member of this racial division, selected from the large number that have fallen under my observation.

(Down, 1866, p. 259)

With the rise of the eugenics movement in the first half of the twentieth century, a number of countries, including certain states in the United States of America, began programmes of forced sterilisation of individuals with Down's syndrome. For example, 'Action T4' was a programme of the systematic murder of individuals with Down's syndrome and other comparable disabilities in Nazi Germany (Lifton, 2000). Since the Second World War, however, laws relating to such sterilisation programmes have been repealed.

In 1961, a number of geneticists wrote to the editor of *The Lancet*, suggesting that Mongolian idiocy had 'misleading connotations', had become 'an embarrassing term', and should be changed (Gordon, 1961). *The Lancet* advocated using the term Down's Syndrome. The World Health Organization (WHO) officially dropped references to mongolism in 1965 after a request by the Mongolian delegate (Howard-Jones, 1979).

Down's syndrome cannot be cured, but the learning and other difficulties associated with it can be addressed if people with the syndrome are offered appropriate help and if other people accept and include. Above all it is important to stress that children with Down's syndrome are individuals and vary in their abilities and achievements. Although they have features in common, they also closely resemble their parents and family. Any one child will only have some of the characteristics associated with Down's syndrome. Each child has a unique appearance, personality and set of abilities. The extent to which a child shows the physical characteristics of the syndrome is no indication of his or her intellectual capacity.

PUPILS WITH PROFOUND AND MULTIPLE LEARNING DISABILITIES

Children with profound and multiple learning disabilities are individual human beings. Some may have autism or Down's syndrome. Others may have Rett syndrome, tuberous sclerosis, Batten's disease or another disorder. One common factor for everyone is that they experience great difficulty communicating. Mencap (undated, p. 4) notes how many people with profound and multiple learning disabilities 'rely on facial expressions, vocal sounds, body language and behaviour to communicate'. Some people may only 'use a small range of formal communication, such as speech, symbols or signs'. Another factor is that learning is likely to be very slow. 'Short-term memory may well be very limited and children may need frequent repetition of the same concepts in the same situations' (ibid.). Some may not reach the stage where they can communicate intentionally. Many may find it hard to understand what others are trying to communicate to them. It is very important, therefore, that those people who support people with profound and multiple learning disabilities 'spend time getting to know their means of communication and finding effective ways to interact with them' (ibid.). Many people will also have additional sensory, physical and/or motor disabilities, or complex health needs.

For very many years there was a general assumption that children with multiple and profound difficulties were ineducable. However, as we saw in Chapter 2, more recently there has been a realisation that they can learn throughout their lives if appropriate support is made available. In England and Wales, for example, the 1970 Education Act acknowledged the right of all children to an appropriate education, irrespective of the degree of difficulty in learning.

ENCOURAGING COMMUNICATION SKILLS IN PUPILS WITH PROFOUND AND MULTIPLE LEARNING DIFFICULTIES

There are a number of ways in which pupils' can be encouraged and supported to communicate with adults and peers, and also electronically.

INTENSIVE INTERACTION

'Intensive Interaction' is aimed at facilitating the development of fundamental social and communication skills for children and young people with the most severe learning difficulties. As Nind (1999) comments, Intensive Interaction is based on the model of 'natural' interactions between caregivers and infants. It is designed to support practitioners to adopt a holistic, nurturing and problem-solving framework for interaction (Yoder, 1990). The teacher (or other practitioner) begins by trying to 'connect' with the learner and developing into 'a familiar repertoire of mutually enjoyable interactive games and playful ritualised routines based on the learner's own preferences'. The teacher or caregiver modifies his/her facial expressions, body language, vocal and gaze behaviours and so on to fit the rhythms of the learner's behaviour. The teacher's/caregiver's behaviour deliberately responds to the learner as if his/her behaviour has 'intentional and communicative significance' (Nind, 1999, p. 97). The repertoire of playful routines provides a safe context for learning the conversational rules of turn taking and mutual interactions (Field, 1979).

The group for whom Intensive Interaction is appropriate may include some children with autism. As Nind (1999) comments, approaches to autism based on ABA assume that learning to communicate can be broken down into sub-tasks that can be taught separately. However, non-directive interactive routes to developing communication skills adopt a different approach. One premise underlying Intensive Interaction is that communication is complex and holistic. Hence Intensive Interaction favours the holistic model of caregiver–infant interaction for encouraging communication skills.

OBJECTS OF REFERENCE AND SYMBOL SYSTEMS

Objects of reference and electronic banks of pictograms are also often used to assist children with varying degrees of cognitive difficulties to communicate.

'Objects of reference' refers to the use of objects to represent those things about which humans communicate: activities, events, people and ideas. These objects can be used as a 'bridge' to more abstract forms of communication such as sign, symbol or word. The contexts in which various objects gain significance and meaning are different for different people. Park (2003) gives the example of Dawn who has learned to use a bottle of bubble bath as her object of reference for 'bath'. He also describes Janet who likes to lie on a trampoline and uses a piece of the cushion material to ask someone to help her climb onto the trampoline in the garden.

AN EXAMPLE OF THE USE OF PICTOGRAMS FOR COMMUNICATION

Widgit Software has produced an array of software programs that use pictorial symbols to support the development of communication skills. In Brunerian terms we might call these 'icons' (see Chapter 4).

Widgit describes its [pictorial] symbol system as follows:

'It is important to understand that *symbols are different from pictures*. We use the word *picture* to describe an illustration in a book, or a drawing on the wall. A picture conveys a lot of information at once and its focus may be unclear, while a symbol focuses on a single concept. This means that symbols can be put together to build more precise information.

Symbol based language and communication has been developed over many years and has a visual structure that supports different parts of speech'.

There are different types of symbols. Symbols are grouped in different sets. The most commonly used across the United Kingdom are Widgit Literacy Symbols (previously known as Rebus) and, according to Widgit, 'are designed to support written information, and provide a way to "translate" written text into a simple and easy to understand form'.

'The Widgit Symbols have a large vocabulary … They have a schematic structure and include grammatical markers for literacy expression'. For example:

The Makaton Vocabulary Development Project has both signs and symbols. 'Makaton is a language programme offering a structured, multi-modal approach, using signs and symbols, for the teaching of communication and language'. For example:

(http://www.widgit.com/index.htm, accessed 28 March 2011, and reprinted with kind permission of Widgit 'Widgit Symbols (c) Widgit Software 2002–2011 www.widgit.com')

THE USE OF INFORMATION AND COMMUNICATIONS TECHNOLOGY (ICT) TO SUPPORT COMMUNICATION

As a number of researchers have noted, Computer-Assisted Learning has the potential to be used as a tool for reducing barriers to learning (Moseley, 1992; Singleton, 1991, 1994; Florian and Hegarty, 2004). Two of these are cognition and communication (Wearmouth, 2009).

Many assistive devices are available to enable students to communicate: electronic language boards, voice synthesisers and voice recognition software. For example 'Lunar Screen Magnifier' is intended to support student who experience visual difficulties to access on-screen text, graphics, tool bars, icons through magnification, colour-changing options, speech and Braille output (http://www.inclusive.co.uk/lunar-screen-magnifier-p1964). 'Hal Screen Reader' is another system that provides screen access for visually impaired computer users through speech output and Braille for users with a Braille display. It includes quick navigation keys, full spelling and attribute announcement, column detection, focus tracking and page scrolling.

Many of the symbol communication systems used by students who experience multiple and profound difficulties in communication are supported by software programs to facilitate writing, as exemplified in Chapter 4. There can be a difficulty in the use of voice recognition software to support the writing of text, however, where students' speech is unclear and their words are not sufficiently differentiated, clear or consistent to be encoded into text.

USING ICT TO SUPPORT YOUNG PEOPLE WITH MULTIPLE AND PROFOUND DIFFICULTIES AND/OR DISABILITIES

Lilley (2004, pp. 82–4) offers a number of examples of an individual programmes developed to incorporate the use of ICT for students with multiple and profound difficulties in learning and/or disabilities. For example, 13-year-old Samantha with cerebral palsy and poor fine and gross motor control was provided with 'an ultra-compact keyboard with guard and a gated joystick' that enabled her to move the cursor on the screen. A large 'jelly-bean' switch replaced the left-click function on a normal mouse. A 'Mouser 3' linked the mouse and the computer to allow switches to be used instead of the mouse buttons. Eleven-year-old Ann was confined to a wheelchair after a road accident when she lost expressive language. A jelly-bean switch was fixed to a specially adapted tray on her wheelchair, and Ann was encouraged to use a range of software programs designed to help learners understand the principle of cause and effect – a press of the switch causes a reaction on the computer screen. When she had mastered simple switch use she was encouraged to work on 'simple scanning software (Clicker 4 – a widely-used piece of software that allows children to click on pictures and phrases which the computer can speak if desired) that can easily be customized' (Lilley, 2004, p. 84).

Use of the Internet appears, as face value, to be a very useful medium for supporting the learning of some students who experience difficulty. Recent developments have come a long way in making access a reality for many students with special learning needs. However, this needs careful consideration of students' special learning needs (Paveley, 2002). Findings from the 1998 National Council for Educational Technology (NCET) project (Wearmouth, 2000, pp. 203–4) indicated that 'real' time access to raw information from the World Wide Web is unrealistic for many students. Interesting or useful web materials often need to be saved on disc for future use. Further, where students are isolated from peers for whatever reason, for example the location of their home, or difficulties with mobility, it may be especially important for students to make contact through e-mail or video-conferencing with peers elsewhere. Use of e-mail provides purpose for reading and writing skills and is highly motivating to students. An e-mail system which integrates the use of a concept keyboard, symbols, a talking word-processor and text, and which automatically deletes headers when messages are received would be useful. However, the way in which students are given choice of e-mail and video-conferencing partners has to be negotiated very carefully.

CONCLUSION

Communication is a vital part of building relationships, sharing experiences and learning. A number of conditions are associated with difficulties in this area, for example PLI, autism and profound and multiple learning difficulties. While it is clearly important to understand the condition in order to respond effectively to children's learning needs, this is only part of the story. Also important is getting to know the individual child, his/her strengths and interests and the wishes of the family.

In Chapter 4 we consider issues related to difficulties in cognition and learning, and some of the ways in which these might be addressed.

4

UNDERSTANDING AND ADDRESSING DIFFICULTIES IN COGNITION AND LEARNING

INTRODUCTION

The chapter will focus on the second of the four broad areas of need: cognition and learning. We have already discussed the issue of profound difficulties in learning in Chapter 3. Here, we look at difficulties more generally and also at one area of what is often called 'specific learning difficulties', that is difficulties that apply to a specific area of learning. Particular attention is given to the kinds of challenges faced by young people identified as experiencing 'moderate' learning difficulties. We go on to discuss one area of need that is often called a 'specific' learning difficulty because it relates to a particular area of learning and not to overall attainment and cognitive ability: dyslexia

UNDERSTANDING COGNITION AND DIFFICULTIES IN COGNITION

The Latin root of the word 'cognition' is 'cognoscere', which means 'to get to know', or 'to recognise'. In general terms, the frame of reference within which 'cognition' is used in the (2001) *Code of practice* relates largely to information-processing associated with problem solving, language, perception and memory and the development of concepts. The cognitive difficulties experienced by some students clearly extend to the area of communication and interaction discussed in Chapter 3. It is obvious, for example, that language acquisition and use are integral to thinking, problem solving and communication (Wearmouth, 2009).

UNDERSTANDING CHILDREN'S MODES OF LEARNING

One very useful frame of reference within which to think about the level of learning at which a child is operating and the difficulty she/ he might be experiencing is Bruner's (1966) model of the different modes of representation of reality used by humans as they develop their conceptual understanding of the world. Bruner (1966) outlines three modes:

- Enactive, that works through action. We 'do' and then we understand and know. It is a mode that works without the need for verbal and/or written and/or physical symbols. In their very early years, young children rely extensively upon enactive modes to learn; as they learn to move, they learn to do so through their own actions. Clearly children unable to experience their world by sight or hearing, taste, touch or smell, or unable to move easily will be less able to understand and know through 'doing' unless special efforts are made to enable them to access their world otherwise;
- Iconic, that works through images that can stand for the physical object. Icons are a visual representation of the real object. Using an iconic mode of representation, children learn to understand what pictures and diagrams are and how to do mathematical calculations using numbers and without counting objects;
- Symbolic, that is an abstract representation of something else. Abstract symbols are 'arbitrary'. Language is a very good example of this. The sound of a word bears no resemblance to reality, unless for example it is onomatopoeic. As Grauberg (2002) notes, one common feature that can be readily identified in children who experience cognitive difficulties is weakness in understanding and remembering that a symbol can 'stand for' something else, for example

something concrete or an action. Where students experience cognitive difficulties, for instance in understanding abstract concepts, teachers might need to build in strategies to classroom teaching which facilitate access to the curriculum in ways that address these difficulties.

Children's learning involves becoming proficient in each of these increasingly more complex modes. They may experience difficulty at any point in their development. Children who experience difficulties in cognition are very likely to need much more time in absorbing concepts using concrete objects and the enactive mode of representation.

MODERATE LEARNING DIFFICULTIES

Although movement through the three modes above can be seen as developmental, it must be said that they are not necessarily age dependent, or invariant. As adults, we habitually use all the three modes (Bruner, 1966).

ADDRESSING MODERATE DIFFICULTIES IN RECEPTIVE LANGUAGE

In Chapter 3, we differentiated between receptive and expressive language skills. Children who experience difficulty in understanding spoken language might learn effectively from teachers who understand that children learn by doing first. The Primary National Strategy [(PNS) 2005, ref 1235/2005] suggests that, whenever possible, pupils should have direct experience of a concept before it is used. Some pupils need time to formulate a reply to a question, so it might be appropriate to forewarn some pupils that they will be asked a question. Some pupils also benefit from being prepared for transitions between different activities and different parts of the classroom and school by, for example, having visual timetables and schedules and being told when and where they are going to move during the school day. Children often get the gist of what is meant from nonverbal clues, so it is important not always to speak in terms that are immediately understood by students otherwise their language will never develop. It is important to ensure that students realise they are being spoken to, and when they are being asked a question. They may need to be taught the skills of whole-class listening.

To ensure that all students understand what is said including those with difficulties in receptive language, as Wearmouth (2009) notes, teachers should check that they speak calmly and evenly, and their faces are clearly visible. They might use visual aids related to the topics being discussed, and explain something several different ways if they have not been understood the first time. They might also make a point of repeating what students say in discussion or question and answer sessions.

STRATEGIES TO DEVELOP ORAL SKILLS

Children will only want to read a text if they can understand what it is that they are reading. To do this they need prior knowledge and experience. Low performance on tests of reading comprehension can also reflect students' limited vocabulary, and/or limited experience in talking about characters and events within stories or concepts of various kinds, and relating these to their own knowledge and experience. Talking is an essential intellectual and social skill that is shaped by how we think and forms part of how we communicate with others and make sense of the world. The young child's thought development begins through interpersonal negotiation with others, caregivers, teachers and peers at school and this is internalised into personal understanding (Vygotsky, 1962). It is clearly very important, therefore, to build up students' oral language skills, by supporting them to talk about what they have been reading and about how what they have been reading connects with what they already know. The potential of a meaningful 'talk to expand literacy' approach that goes beyond studying letters and words is supported by a number of research studies.

From the time a child first begins to understand the world she/he appears to do so by means of story. 'Any understanding we have of reality is in terms of our stories and our story-creating possibilities' (Mair, 1988, p. 128). Sarbin (1986) notes that it is through story that children learn to become functioning members of the society into which they are born.

> It is through hearing stories ... that children learn or mislearn both what a child and what a parent is, what the cast of characters may be

in the drama into which they have been born and what the ways of the world are.

There is no way to enable children to understand society 'except through the stock of stories which constitute its initial dramatic resources'. If children are deprived of stories 'you leave them unscripted, anxious stutterers in their actions as in their words' (Sarbin, 1986, p. 201).

There is an important question about how learners can take the step 'from speaking to understanding writing on a page or screen, to realise that knowledge of life and language can help them make sense of words and texts' (Gregory, 1996, p. 95). Orally told stories, rhymes, songs, prayer and routines for meeting and greeting people, all have an important role in literacy acquisition and are promoted within many cultures long before children begin any form of formal education. Gregory (1996, p. 112) advocates addressing the issue of building from the known into new literacy acquisition by explicit scaffolding of children's learning through 'recognising children's existing linguistic skills and cultural knowledge' and then deliberately 'building these into both teaching content and teaching strategies'. She describes a reading session that draws on children's oral language and makes use of puppets to mediate learning. This should draw on the child's emotions, for example fear, love, sympathy, hate and aim to tell an adventure or drama. Well-chosen stories told in the classroom by the teacher can scaffold children's learning about written texts in a way that conversation cannot. Chapters for reading should include 'memorable stories and texts from all times and places', perhaps containing 'universal truths, values and morals, fear and security' which relate to pupils of all levels and ages (ibid., p. 122). Ways in which beginning readers might be introduced to story-reading sessions include explicitly discussing the context for the story, one or more of the characters, and the plot, reading the story slowly, clearly, with 'lively intonation' and without interruption, discussing the story and the themes, and relating these to the children's lives. Gregory (1996, p. 120) gives an example of a text, 'The Clay Flute' by Mats Rehnman, that seems complex but is popular with children. It is set in the Arabian Desert and tells the story of a poor boy who suffers many misfortunes but finally 'makes good'. The language is difficult but rich in imagery and emotive vocabulary (witch, horrible, grab, scream, kiss, tear, sword, heart, etc.).

Gregory identifies the reasons for its popularity as its clear purpose in the way the plot develops, its portrayal of the universal values of courage and kindness and the way good is seen to triumph over evil.

UNDERSTANDING WRITTEN TEXT

Having the ability to handle written text with confidence is a key part of coping with the day-to-day expectations of life. Commonly, difficulties in receptive language may include barriers relating to reading comprehension.

DEVELOPING READING COMPREHENSION

First, it is important to be able to judge the level of difficulty of any text used in class, for example sentence length and complexity, word length and familiarity and the degree of conciseness in the explanation of concepts. It is also important to consider carefully (Lunzer and Gardner, 1979) the interest level of the text and/or prior knowledge of the subject matter. If students are interested in what they are reading or are familiar with the subject material, they can cope with more difficult text. Further, more students can understand higher level concepts if ideas are expanded and explained step by step.

Strategies for developing reading comprehension can include adding pictures, subheadings and summaries to the text and teaching students to take notes, underline key passages or write summaries. Students can be taught to scan the text before reading in depth, including focusing on pictures, diagrams, captions, subheadings and highlighted words (Wearmouth, 2009, pp. 42–3). They can be taught to think consciously about the text as they read: whether it fits in with what they already know, whether they have understood it or what questions they might ask themselves about the meaning of a text as they read it through. The amount read before questions are raised can be shortened. This may mean a page by page reading, or even a paragraph by paragraph reading. Close consideration must be given to the constitution of student groups in this case. As students pay more attention to the messages conveyed by text the amount of text read before questions are asked can be lengthened. Groups of students can be encouraged to share the reading of a book and then discuss topics such as: how did the main character feel? has anything like this ever happened to you?; what happens next? Cloze can be used to make sure that students are reading for meaning. Here every fifth word or so is deleted from the text, and the student is asked to fill in the gaps with a suitable, meaningful word.

Often students need to gain more experience in reading in order to increase word identification, knowledge of letter/sound combinations and use of contextual information and inference (Duke and Pearson, 2002). Excellent ways in which to develop these skills and also the related writing skills of language structure, organisation of thought and creative writing are following the text with the eyes while listening to a recording (which has to be word-perfect), 'paired reading' or 'reading buddies'.

ICT SUPPORT FOR READING

The use of symbols on some computer programmes acts as scaffolding for reading. Symbols can be used with one student and gradually withdrawn until she/he can read without them. The left–right directionality of reading can be reinforced through the *Clicker* programme (Crick Software). Sound to support reading and writing can be used in many different ways. Word processors with speech synthesis can be very powerful. Learners can hear what they have written, either as they are writing, or hear the whole text after they have finished.

Sound can be introduced to text by dropping it into a standard text to speech utility or talking word processor. The text may also be dropped into a programme such as *Writing with Symbols* (Widgit computing), which gives a symbolic version that can be printed out and spoken aloud. Talking word processors may be particularly useful tools to enable students to decode text downloaded from the Internet.

An example of a programme to develop switch-accessible stories and slide shows is 'SwitchIt! Maker 2'. Each activity has a sequence of on-screen pages that can have a picture, video or text-based material, music or recorded speech. Pages can be turned by a simple switch, the computer's spacebar, the mouse buttons or IntelliKeys.

EXPRESSIVE LANGUAGE

Students who experience difficulty in expressing themselves need frequent opportunities for exploratory talk in every area of the curriculum in order to put new information and ideas into their own words and link subject matter to what they already know. Strategies that facilitate oral language development might include exploratory talk in small groups, problem-solving aloud, explanations of how something is made, or how and why things happen, dramatisation and roleplay, interviews (live or taped) and group discussion.

WRITING

Learners who experience problems in expressing themselves in writing may often benefit from structured support to help them develop skills for different types of writing. Allowing a student to dictate text onto an audio recorder and then transcribing it for him/her will help him/her to get thoughts and ideas down on paper. Alternatively, the student can be allowed to dictate text while the teacher/older student/parent scribes.

Using ICT can also facilitate writing for some pupils. Word processing can offer

> a means of drafting and re-drafting that is easy, efficient and accessible and so is a great equaliser in presentation.... Pupils can work more quickly and demonstrate different types of writing exercise and have the opportunity to experiment ... and thus demonstrate their true ability.
>
> (Lilley, 2004, p. 89)

An example of a writing support and multimedia tool for children of all abilities is 'Clicker' (http://www.cricksoft.com/uk/products/clicker/guide.htm, accessed 30 November 2010). At the top of the screen is a word processor called 'Clicker Writer'. At the bottom of the screen is the 'Clicker Grid'. This has 'cells' containing letters, words or phrases that teachers can click on, to send them into Clicker Writer so that students can write sentences without actually writing or using the keyboard.

ENGLISH AS AN ADDITIONAL LANGUAGE AND SPECIAL EDUCATIONAL NEEDS

The Special Educational Needs Code of Practice notes that the identification and assessment of the special educational needs of young people whose first language is not English requires particular care. Lack of competence in English cannot be equated with general difficulties in learning, or particular difficulties in language acquisition as understood in this Code. Students learning English may say little or nothing for some time, but are learning nevertheless.

There is no possibility of making sense of what bears no relation to one's own ways of making sense of things. Unfamiliarity with local culture, customs and language on entering school can result in complete bewilderment and an inability to understand the expectations and norms of the literacy curriculum. Gregory (1996, p. 33) notes, for example, how 'Tony' arrived at school, aged 4 years and 10 months, with an 'eye for detail' and a 'disciplined and structured approach to reading from his Chinese school'. In his Chinese school he had been 'given an exercise book where he had to divide the page into columns and practise ideographs over and over again until they are perfect' (ibid., p. 32). The carefully and clearly delineated and constrained tasks set by the previous teacher contrasted sharply with the range of personal choice given to 'Tony' and his classmates in the mainstream classroom in Northampton, England. His aimless wandering around the classroom while peers chose activities for themselves indicated that he appeared unable to cope with the non-realisation of his expectations about what school should be about.

Having said this, we cannot assume that their language status of unfamiliar or conflicting expectations is the only reason for students who learn English as an additional language to make slow progress. They may also experience general cognitive difficulties. This may be a very sensitive area that requires specialist help.

MEMORY PROBLEMS

Within the area of moderate learning difficulties, very poor memory is a problem for a number of students. There are a number of common reasons for this. For example, students may not have grasped of the information clearly in the first place. They may not have linked the new information to previous knowledge sufficiently. Or they may not have distinguished new knowledge from what is already known, so that the new information interferes with the old. It may therefore not be a good idea to introduce concepts with clear similarities together. For example, if we were to introduce a donkey and a pony at the same time and tell the child that the donkey is the one with the big ears, it may be that the child is forever afterwards confused about which is which.

There are a number of frames of reference against which to conceptualise what happens in the human memory system. In one, memory is seen as having two distinctive parts: long-term memory and short-term or 'working' memory. Long-term memory itself is also often seen as consisting of two parts: knowing *that* (declarative or semantic memory), and knowing *how* (procedural memory). There is clearly a big difference between knowing a fact, for example a date, and knowing how to do something. Memory can be accessed through recall or through recognition. Of these, recognition is usually easier than recall, although if the context in which the initial learning occurred is very similar to the context in which recall is needed and there are strong memory cues, then recall can be easier.

Many students with short-term memory difficulties have problems in absorbing and recalling information or responding to and carrying out instructions within a busy classroom situation. They may find it difficult to copy from the blackboard as they are unable to memorise what they have seen and transpose it to the paper on the desk. In addition to this they are required to rotate this visual image through 90 degrees from the vertical to the horizontal and also to transpose the size of the letters involved. Young children have to learn sequences of certain items relating to particular areas that are important for everyday living, for example letters of the alphabet, months of the year, days of the week and numbers. There are many students who, even in secondary schools, cannot recite either the alphabet or the months of the year in the correct order.

Difficulties in this area, however, can be improved with training. Teachers and/or families might try increasing the span of items that are to be remembered and the length of time between presenting the sequence and asking for recall. As memory span increases, an intervening task can be given between presentation and recall. They might also try gradually increasing sequences of instructions, beginning with one or two only: 'Please go to the cupboard and get some pencils', and subsequently, perhaps: 'Please go to the cupboard, get some pencils, give one to Jane and one to Aaron'. They could ask the student to give a verbal message to deliver to another teacher, secretary, administrator and increasing the length of the message as the student is successful. It is important to encourage the student to repeat the instruction before carrying it out and use his/her own voice to aid his/her memory. After reading a short story, they could make a point of asking the student to identify the main characters, sequence of events and outcome. They might also encourage students to think up their own mnemonic and visualisation techniques and, if possible, both together, or repeat aloud and rehearse items to be remembered, and use a multi-sensory mode of learning through oral, visual, auditory and kinaesthetic activities. The learner should be able to see, hear, say and, if possible, touch the materials to be learned. This reinforces the input stimuli and helps to consolidate the information for use, meaning and transfer to other areas. Teachers can keep verbal instructions clear and concise and ensure student is attending before teachers start to speak. It can help to preface instructions with a warning (e.g. Peter, in a moment I am going to ask you) to ensure that the student is ready to listen. They might also encourage students to repeat back key points as well as to talk through tasks as their own voice to help to direct their motor movements, and try supplementing auditory verbal material with visual cues and practical demonstrations. In some cases, written checklists or pictorial reminders may be beneficial (Wearmouth, 2009, p. 48).

DIFFICULTIES EXPERIENCED IN THE LEARNING OF MATHEMATICS

Much teaching and assessment in the area of mathematics takes place in the context of a symbolic representation of mathematics, that is, through written text and pictures (J. Rogers, 2007, p. 2). Many children appear to adopt mathematical symbols and algorithms without having grasped the concepts that underpin them (Borthwick and Harcourt-Heath, 2007). While activities involving reading and writing numbers may tell us something about children's ability to read and write numbers, they do not necessarily tell us anything about children's conceptual understanding of 'numberness'. Learners' ability to understand symbolic representation depends on understanding of the first-hand experience to which the symbolic representation refers. In the case of younger learners this may involve, for example, the handling and counting of everyday items. Learning to use number symbols is likely to occur simultaneously with acquiring the alphabetic principle and sound-symbol correspondence in literacy acquisition and, as Grauberg (2002) comments, 'Where is the "f" in 5?' It is possible to use other number systems, for example tally charts, first, where one bundle represents five and clearly made up of five. Rogers (2007, p. 13) notes that a weak conceptual framework for understanding number in the early years on which to begin formal mathematics teaching

> make it both difficult to engage children (Department of Education and Science, 1989) and to correct later (Nunes & Bryant, 1997). It is also well documented that such difficulties soon become compounded, resulting in distress and further delay (Adult Literacy and Basic Skills Unit, 1992). Attention needs to be paid to the negative effects of incomprehension of a prominent part of the mathematics curriculum in which young children are involved on a daily basis. It may be that such incomprehension prompts the early lack of confidence in mathematics that characterises further failure and poor problem-solving during the later school years. They can often learn to count up and down 'in ones' and can take part in counting games and activities. However, understanding that a number, for example five, is not just the last number in the series 15 (the ordinal principle), but also means the whole set of five (the principle of cardinality) is another matter.

Pictorial symbols or icons are clearly different from abstract symbols used at the symbolic stage of reasoning in Bruner's framework. If we take the example of mathematics learning in schools, lack of symbolic understanding can lead to difficulties in the written recording of number work, relational signs: 'plus', 'minus', 'equal(s)', place value and 'zero', money and time, as Grauberg (2002, p. 5) notes.

RELATIONAL SIGNS: 'PLUS', 'MINUS', 'EQUAL(S)'

Adding and subtracting both imply actions. Without an understanding of what the action is there is little point in trying to encourage the use of the symbol. '=' is often interpreted to children as 'makes', but, as we are all aware, a child's notion of 'makes' is clearly not what the symbol '=' means, mathematically.

Very great care must be taken in working out ways to support children's understanding by making clear links from one small step to the next. Primary schools in particular have a lot of equipment that can be used to play games in adding, subtracting and balancing.

Bearing in mind Bruner's three modes of representation, for some children it might be important to use concrete aids to establish number learning, for example Cuisenaire rods and/or an abacus, for much longer than for other children. A major question is how to move from the act of adding, taking away or balancing to competent use of the abstract symbols. One way to do this might be to spend time thinking about ways in which children will move into and through the iconic mode of representation and to encourage children to devise their own symbols for the actions first so that the icon visibly represents their own understandings.

COMMON PROBLEMS: THE EXAMPLES OF PLACE VALUE AND 'ZERO'

Difficulties with the concept of place value and 'zero' can be experienced by students to the end of their secondary education.

COMMON CONCEPTUAL DIFFICULTIES IN MATHEMATICS

As the head of learning support in an upper (13–18) school I observed numbers of students in mainstream lessons struggling with mathematical concepts that regular mainstream teachers assumed they had grasped a long time before. In their mathematics lessons I was still trying to support them to develop a basic understanding of place value. In other areas of the curriculum they were expected to cope with the concept of hundreds, thousands and millions which they found so frustratingly complex and difficult that their behaviour became disruptive. An example is geography or social studies lessons where population density was expressed in thousands per square mile. Some students could not handle the concepts of thousands and millions competently and confidently, either in an ordinal or cardinal sense, and became very frustrated.

Zero is another problematic concept, mathematically. I was once asked by 14-year-old students in a mixed comprehensive school how nought multiplied by a number could possibly equal nought. How could a number suddenly equal nothing? 'I replied by taking a handful of nothing and putting it down on the desk 44 times to prove the point' (Wearmouth, 2009, p. 138).

Without understanding the whole concept of place value the use of zero as a place holder in a multi-digit line is difficult to comprehend for some students. One way to start to address problems with place value might be to continue to use concrete equipment such as Dienes materials – unit cubes, 'longs' of 10 cm cubes, and 'flats' of 100 cm cubes – for much longer than the teacher might have anticipated, providing that this can be done without embarrassing the child(ren). For example, 54 might be written down at first as 50 with the 4 superimposed over the 0, and 504 would be written down as 500 with the 4 superimposed over the last 0. Alternatively, as Grauberg (2002) notes, the numbers may be written on transparencies and then superimposed.

UNDERSTANDING NUMBERNESS

Teaching number in the early years through the use of number sequences seems to be common in the United Kingdom and the United States (Grauberg, 2002). In some other countries in Europe and the Far East, for example Japan, the preference is for emphasising recognition of small quantities without counting. Recognising a small number, for example four, as a quantity involves one operation of matching a sound symbol or visual symbol to an amount. This seems, logically, easier than recognising four from a number sequence. This latter involves remembering that four comes after three and before five, and simultaneously counting up to the total amount. It will take a lot of concrete activities in a variety of different contexts before a child with cognitive difficulties understands the concept of 'numberness':

> ... which means the concept of 'twoness', 'threeness', 'nness'. Through his [sic] experience with many different materials we want him to see what is common to all (the fact that there are, for instance, 'two' of each) and we want him to learn to ignore what is irrelevant (e.g. size, colour, feel).
>
> (Ibid., p. 12)

TIME

'Time' is a complex concept for children to develop. As Piaget (1969) notes, it includes points in time, duration and sequence of events, frequency of events and intervals between them.

Concepts of time vary, as Grauberg (2002) points out. Supporting a student to acquire a concept of time is a very different proposition from teaching him/her to tell the time. There is no constant point of reference in relation to many indicators of time. 'Late' can refer to a time in the morning, if a student should have arrived earlier, or to a point at night when, for example, that student could be early or on time. Our sense of the passage of time is not constant either. It often seems to distort depending on the activity and our engagement with, or enjoyment of, it. For example, the few days before a birthday often seem to young children to pass much more slowly than most other days.

Bruner's three modes of representation – enactive, iconic and symbolic – again offer a framework for thinking about activities and approaches for students who experience difficulties in the acquisition of time-related concepts. Using a timer or some sort might help in the initial stages to enact the representation of time passing. Concentrating on the sounds emitted on striking a percussion instrument themselves might encourage a sense of the frequency of events. To encourage the concept of sequence, a teacher might first organise an activity for children to act out a regular sequence of events in their own lives and then represent sequence pictorially (Bruner's iconic mode of representation). These days the concept of a visual timetable for use in schools with young children and older children who experience cognitive difficulties is quite common (Selikowitz, 2008).

To tell the time, use of a digital timer is a simpler option than a traditional clock face. However, there are other considerations. The hands of the traditional clock face can be seen to move in the context of the 12-hour cycle, but the numbers on a digital timepiece simply move (Wearmouth, 2009).

SPECIFIC LEARNING DIFFICULTIES

Some young people experience difficulties in learning in specific areas that appear to be unrelated to their overall ability. One of these areas of difficulty is often linked to the concept of dyslexia.

THE EXAMPLE OF DYSLEXIA

'Dyslexia' is a concept about which there is much controversy. Some of this relates to whether or not there is an identifiable entity that we might term 'dyslexia' and, if so, what its precise nature, causes and explanations might be (Stanovich, 2000). Some concerns best practice in identification, assessment and teaching. There are also issues of equity in resourcing individual learning needs by privileging certain groups of students. One of the 'major' tensions in dyslexia research results from the potential conflict between the different agenda of individual and interest groups: researchers and practitioners, parents and teachers, teachers and educational psychologists, schools and local authorities and local authorities and governments (Fawcett, 2002). The issue of funding provision for individual dyslexic students can force the various interest groups into opposition, for example.

'Dyslexia' is a psychological explanation of difficulties in learning. The information-processing system of 'dyslexic' individuals is seen as different from that of non-dyslexics in ways which have an impact on a number of areas of performance. Pumfrey (1996) describes dyslexia as a 'variable syndrome', implying that definitions of dyslexia may vary and be interpreted in different ways. Some definitions relate only to difficulty in acquiring literacy as reflected by its derivation from Classical Greek: δυσ (dys), meaning 'bad' or 'difficult', and λεξίς (lexis), meaning 'word', or 'speech'. Other definitions are wider and include reference to difficulties in co-ordination, personal organisation, balance, patterning, directionality (right/left confusion), sequencing, rhythm, orientation, memory and so on.

In terms of literacy acquisition, the difficulties experienced by dyslexic students are usually related to difficulties in processing either visual or/and auditory information and making the connections between the visual symbols and the sounds they represent, commonly called 'decoding'. In relation to visual factors, learners may experience difficulty in any of the following areas (Wearmouth, 2009): recognition of the visual cues of letters and words, familiarity with left–right orientation, recognition of word patterns and recognition of letter and word shapes. Or they may encounter problems with any of the following auditory factors: recognition of letter sounds, recognition of sounds and letter groups or patterns, sequencing of sounds, corresponding sounds to visual stimuli, discriminating sounds from other sounds and/or discriminating sounds within words. The British Psychological Society (BPS) working party adopted this narrower view of dyslexia related solely to literacy:

> Dyslexia is evident when accurate and fluent reading and or spelling develops very incompletely or with great difficulty. This focuses on literacy learning at the 'word level' and implies that the problem is severe and persistent despite appropriate learning opportunities. It provides the basis for a staged process of assessment through teaching.
>
> (BPS, 1999, p. 18)

The wider definition of the British Dyslexia Association (BDA) includes difficulty in the development of literacy and language-related skills, particularly in phonological processing, and also in working memory, the speed of processing information and the automatic development of skills that may not reflect the level of other cognitive abilities. 'Conventional' teaching methods may not be suffice in addressing such difficulties but information technology and individual counselling may lessen the effects (http://www.bdadyslexia.org.uk/about-dyslexia/further-information/dyslexia-research-information-.html).

The Rose review on identifying and teaching dyslexic children concurs with this wider view (Rose, 2009, p. 30). This review identifies dyslexia as a learning difficulty associated with 'difficulties in phonological awareness, verbal memory and verbal processing speed' that not only 'affects the skills involved in accurate and fluent word reading and spelling' but also acknowledges a wider range of information-processing difficulties in various 'aspects of language, motor co-ordination, mental calculation, concentration and personal organisation'. However, these aspects alone are not markers of dyslexia. A 'good indication' is the extent to which 'the individual responds or has responded to well-founded intervention'. In other words, as the BPS (1999) implies also, if a child experiences difficulties but has not received good teaching, then it cannot be assumed that she/he is dyslexic.

ASSOCIATION BETWEEN DYSLEXIA AND INTELLIGENCE

One debate around dyslexia relates to whether a child is dyslexic if his/her difficulties in literacy can be attributed to general low ability.

Two methods used to identify dyslexia, both of which utilise IQ, can be compared to highlight the implications for practice: the 'cut-off method' and the 'regression' method. Both have resource implications for the type of teaching programmes and provision allocated. The regression method essentially looks at the discrepancy between IQ and the reading level that would be *predicted* based on a child's IQ score. This means that a child with a high IQ score who may be around or only slightly below his age level in reading can still be identified as dyslexic because the reading level may still be below that expected for the IQ level. On the other hand, the cut-off method means that any child with an average or above IQ but is lagging in their reading level by at least 18 months can be described as dyslexic. As the BPS (1999, p. 67) notes, both these methods can be problematic for two reasons. Both rely on the validity of the IQ measure as a robust indicator of a child's abilities. Also, measures of IQ and reading ages can change over time and a child who qualifies for additional help on account of any of these measures may make an improvement in reading which would exclude them, using the discrepancy criteria, from continuing to use the label dyslexia or qualify for extra help. In practice, therefore, a child receiving additional help may lose this support if she/he makes gain which narrows the discrepancy gap between reading and IQ.

EFFECTS ON PERFORMANCE

Riddick *et al.* (2002, pp. 12–13) describes how dyslexia affects young children's performance in various areas. At preschool level there may be a delay in spoken language, including difficulty in learning nursery rhymes and verbal sequencing, for example days of the week and letters of the alphabet. There may also be poor gross motor co-ordination, for example in learning to ride a bicycle or swim, poor fine motor skills, for example in copying shapes and letters, and poor short-term memory, for example remembering a sequence of instructions and/or names. At primary age a child is likely to experience difficulties in reading, writing, spelling and number work. The child may be unable to identify rhythm and alliteration, or read single words accurately. She/he may reverse some words, for example 'pot' and 'top', miss out whole lines and read some sections of text twice without realising it and have better understanding of text than word accuracy. Reading age for fluency and accuracy is likely to be below chronological age. Children who begin school with poor letter knowledge and poor rhythmic ability may be at risk of developing difficulties in reading. Snowling (2000, pp. 213–14), for example, says that difficulties in encoding the phonological features of words (i.e. the sound system of a language) is core to dyslexic children's difficulties.

> Dyslexia is a specific form of language impairment that affects the way in which the brain encodes the phonological features of spoken words. The core deficit is in phonological processing ... Dyslexia specifically affects the development of reading and spelling skills.

A child may spell the same word different ways in the same text, spell incorrectly words learnt for spelling tests, make several attempts to spell words with frequent crossings out, spell phonetically but incorrectly, use what look like bizarre spellings for example 'bidar' for 'because', leave out syllables, for example 'onge' for 'orange, or part of a letter blend especially when there is a blend of three letters, for example 'sred' for 'shred', reverse letters, especially 'b' and 'd', 'p' and 'q'. She/he may experience difficulty copying from the board, produce work that is chaotic or very untidy, begin writing anywhere on the page, confuse upper and lower case letters, produce very little output and what there is may be unintelligible even to the child.

Dyslexic children experience a number of difficulties in mathematics including the learning of number bonds and multiplication tables, the understanding of concepts involving directionality (Weavers, 2003). Time and spatial concepts can prove difficult. Children may find sequencing activities and orientation or both numbers and processes hard. Confusion can arise through having to process different operations in different directions, for example the conventional right to left calculation of addition and subtraction, and left to right of division. There may be limited spatial awareness and visual discrimination, resulting in confusion of signs and reversal of digits. Children may also have very poor mental arithmetic (mental manipulation of number/symbols in short-term memory) (Wearmouth, 2009).

ADDRESSING DIFFICULTIES EXPERIENCED BY PRIMARY-AGED DYSLEXIC PUPILS IN MATHEMATICS

Riddick *et al.* (2002, p. 50) offer a number of suggestions about teaching such students:

- make sure they understand basic symbols = + − etc.;
- make sure they understand basic number language for example subtract, multiply, etc.;
- repeat learning and revision of number facts;
- teach child to estimate a sensible answer;
- teach child to check their answer against the set question;
- be alert for reversals which lead to child making a wrong calculation;
- practise counting forwards and backwards in sequences, for example in ones, then two, and so on;
- use pattern methods to teach number bonds;
- teach multiplication using table squares;
- use squared paper to aid correct setting out of calculations;
- give a sample strip with digits in correct orientation for checking reversals;
- use multi-sensory teaching; rehearse what has just been learnt with oral revision at the end of the lesson;
- teach using logic rather than just rules so conceptual ability can be utilised.

At secondary level, students may become withdrawn, subdued, anxious about reading out loud or taking written tests, socially isolated and experience psychosomatic difficulties, for example sickness and headaches (Riddick *et al.*, 2002). She/he is likely also to feel very tired because of the exertion involved in trying to cope with increasing literacy demands (Wearmouth, 2004).

THEORIES EXPLAINING DYSLEXIA

There are a number of theories that attempt to explain the difficulties experienced by dyslexic learners.

VISUAL-BASED THEORIES

As Everatt (2002) explains, there are visual-based theories which propose that dyslexia may be the consequence of an abnormality in the neural pathways of the visual system. There are others suggesting a lower level of activity in the areas of the visual cortex thought to be responsible for identifying the direction of movement (Eden *et al.*, 1996). There is also a view that visual difficulties may be caused by oversensitivity to certain wavelengths (or colours) of light. This is sometimes referred to as scotopic sensitivity syndrome (Irlen, 1991). The significance of this is that coloured filters, overlays or lenses which are said to alleviate reading problems for some learners (Wilkins *et al.*, 1994) have increasingly been incorporated into teachers' practice, with variable results.

CEREBELLAR DEFICIT HYPOTHESIS

Nicolson and Fawcett (1994) developed the cerebellar deficit hypothesis in order to account for common patterns of difficulties among individuals identified as 'dyslexic: problems in balance, speed and phonological skill. The cerebellum is a densely packed and deeply folded subcortical brain structure, also known as the "hind brain"' (Fawcett and Nicholson, 2001). In humans, it accounts for 10–15 per cent of brain weight, 40 per cent of brain surface area and 50 per cent of the brain's neurones. Damage to different parts of the cerebellum can lead to different symptoms in humans ranging from disturbances in posture and balance, to limb rigidity, loss of muscle tone, lack of co-ordination and impaired timing of rapid pre-planned automatic movements.

The results of a number of studies investigating the role of the cerebellum and its implications for dyslexia (Fawcett *et al.*, 1996; Nicolson and Fawcett, 1999; Finch *et al.*, 2002) indicate that dyslexic children showed, first, clinical symptoms of cerebellar abnormality. Also, there were abnormalities in cerebellar activation in automatic processing and in new learning. Greater frontal lobe activation suggested they were bypassing the cerebellum to some extent. Overall this indicates that dyslexic children may use different methods in sequential learning and automatic performance. Fawcett and Nicolson hypothesise that the causal chain between cerebellar problems, phonological difficulties and eventual reading problems accounts for three criterial difficulties of dyslexia: writing, reading and spelling.

THE 'BALANCE MODEL' OF READING AND DYSLEXIA

The 'Balance Model' of reading and dyslexia is another example of a biological model (Robertson and Bakker, 2002). The balance model hypothesises that early and advanced reading, that is, reading through decoding and attention to perceptual features of text, and reading for meaning, are mediated by the right and left hemisphere of the brain respectively. This model predicts that some children, P (perceptual)-type dyslexics, rely too much on the perceptual features of text and may not be able to shift from right to left in the hemispheric mediation of reading. Some other children, L (linguistic)-type dyslexics, rely on linguistic features of text to read fast and construct meaning, but pay too little attention to perceptual features of text.

The results of these investigations indicate that P- and L-dyslexics differ with regard to the speed of processing of reading-related information. P-types are faster than L-types in deciding whether all letters in an array are the same or different but P-types are slower than L-types when it comes to the question whether a word is real or not (Licht, 1994; Bakker, 1990; Fabbro *et al.*, 2001).

The allocation to sub-types is based largely on observation of pupil performance in the particular aspects of the reading process which are causing concern (Robertson and Bakker, 2002). Intervention therefore can aim to directly adapt learning behaviour in line with the identified weaknesses in reading behaviour.

PHONOLOGICAL DEFICIT HYPOTHESIS

Since the 1980s being the dominant, theory used to explain dyslexia has been the phonological deficit hypothesis (Bradley and Bryant, 1983; Snowling, 2000; Stanovich, 2000). Phonological representations can be interpreted as the knowledge about sounds which a reader brings to the task of reading. Phonological processing is strongly related to the development of reading. Difficulties experienced at the level of phonological representation and the relationships between symbols and the sounds they represent constrain reading development. Hatcher and Snowling (2002) comment that one of the effects of this is that learners who experience difficulties at the phonological level are less able to generalise knowledge about the phonological properties of sounds and words they are taught. Activities such as non-word reading are problematic because of the difficulties associated with sound–symbol relationships. Hatcher and Snowling feel that this can be viewed as one of the most robust signs of dyslexia.

Hatcher and Snowling suggest that the most crucial factor in the individual profile of dyslexic children is the severity of the lack of development in phonological representations. This can account for the differences between dyslexic children's profiles and the different presenting characteristics of the dyslexic group. Additionally dyslexic children with poorer phonological representations will have fewer compensatory word attack strategies to draw on and this will further undermine their reading performance.

Hatcher and Snowling conclude that assessment of phonological skills is therefore necessary by, for example, providing examples of tasks: rhyme recognition, rhyme production, phonological manipulation such as phoneme deletion and letter knowledge, which can be found in some of the established tests available for this purpose. This view has considerable implications for intervention programmes in the early years.

ADDRESSING DIFFICULTIES ASSOCIATED WITH DYSLEXIA

In their review of dyslexia, Rice and Brooks (2004) conclude that research appears not to indicate that 'dyslexics' and 'ordinary poor readers' should be taught by different methods. The same kind of approaches to addressing reading, writing and mathematical difficulties that are appropriate for dyslexic learners can also be useful for other students.

Teaching approaches for dyslexic students can be grouped into those that are designed to enable the child to overcome the difficulties that are experienced as far as possible – almost to train the personal information-processing system to become more organised in a deliberately systematic and focused way (personal reflections) – and those that enable the child to cope.

PHONOLOGICAL AWARENESS TRAINING

When children are very young it may be difficult for them to realise that speech can be broken down into individual words or that words can also be broken down into sounds. Phonemic awareness develops only when there is good experience of speaking and listening. It can be encouraged by playing rhyming games, making up nonsense rhymes, repeating rhyming strings and playing other games which require the manipulation of sounds. Hatcher and Snowling (2002) outline examples of phonological awareness training such as rhyme activities, identifying words as units within sentences, syllable awareness and blending tasks.

As Hatcher and Snowling comment, while it is important to train phonological awareness it is also important to establish the relationship between sounds and written forms of words. Interventions that rely exclusively on training in phonological awareness are less effective than those that combine phonological training with print and meaning in the context of sentences in text. Interventions that address difficulties in co-ordination, personal organisation, directionality, balance and patterning may also be needed for some students.

ACQUISITION OF FLUENCY IN READING AND WRITING

At almost any age, paired reading arrangements can enable dyslexic individuals to gain more experience in reading ('reading mileage'; Clay, 1993, 1998) to enable greater experience in reading and in visual tracking of the text in order to increase word identification, knowledge of letter/sound combinations and use of contextual information and inference. Students might be encouraged to choose reading material of high interest to themselves, irrespective of its readability level, and both children might read out loud together, with the reading partner modulating his/her speed to match that of the dyslexic pupil. Or children might be encouraged to use recordings of books that they really want to read, tracking through the text with their eyes while listening to the CD.

In terms of writing, allowing students to dictate his/her thoughts onto a digital recorder and then transcribing them for him/her, or allowing him/her to dictate thoughts to the teacher/an older child/ the parent, in the first instance is a coping strategy. Encouraging the child to listen to the recording of his/her own thoughts and then write the text from this is one way to separate out the conceptual thinking around content and the mechanical aspects of writing with which the child is likely to experience difficulty.

Pupils might also be provided with writing frames to support extended writing and encourage logical sequencing (Wray, 2002).

MULTI-SENSORY APPROACHES TO LEARNING

As we also saw in Chapter 3, multi-sensory approaches are a very important way to harnessing all the senses to support students' learning. Introducing visual, tactile, auditory and kinaesthetic modes to teaching and learning enables students who need extra reinforcement in their learning to see, touch, hear and move, sometimes simultaneously, in their learning activities. The principles of multi-sensory teaching which apply to language work also apply to the mathematics field, for example, introducing new mathematical concepts and processes using concrete materials, diagrams, pictures and verbal explanation. Progress should be carefully monitored at each stage, checking that a particular concept has been thoroughly mastered and understood before moving on to the next step.

'METACOGNITIVE' STRATEGIES

'Metacognitive' strategies can also help dyslexic and other students to think about their own thinking processes so that those who experience difficulty in particular areas of learning can develop alternative routes to accessing these areas. 'Mind-mapping' (Buzan, 2000) that encourages learners first to produce a visual representation of all those areas to be covered in the text before beginning on the written task is an example of one way to develop a structure for producing extended text.

COPING STRATEGIES

Research (Florian and Hegarty, 2004) stresses the motivational value of computer-assisted learning, for example word processing which can increase the time that students are willing to practise writing. Spell-checkers can remove much of a pupil's inhibition about writing that comes from poor spelling. Drafting and correcting becomes less laborious and the printed copy can be corrected away from the machine by the student or the teacher and improved versions created without difficulty. Everything can be saved and reused easily, allowing work to be done in small amounts. Presentation is improved; when the final version is printed it is legible and well presented.

Optical comfort is also important. A choice of screen colours can be helpful to students.

VISUAL DISCRIMINATION/SPATIAL ANALYSIS

Strategies to enable pupils to cope with particular difficulties in the area of spatial analysis and visual discrimination in the classroom might include keeping all visually presented materials simple in format and uncluttered by excessive stimuli and assisting the student in planning and organising assigned tasks written on paper by providing visual cues and providing step-by-step instructions (Wearmouth, 2009). When giving directions it is often helpful for teachers and others to be specific and use concrete cues. New concepts might be introduced where appropriate by beginning with the identification of individual parts and moving to integrated wholes.

EXAMINATION CONCESSIONS

The school might give internal examination concessions (extra time, answers in note form, oral test to support written examination, use of word processor in course work, examinations, etc.) and 25 per cent additional time. Examination papers might be duplicated so that the pupil can see both sides of a page at the same time, enlarged or printed on coloured paper, along with the use of highlighting pens to help with the analysis of questions.

MARKING STUDENTS' WORK

In school, there may be considerable difference of opinion about the extent to which corrections should be made to a script which contains very many mistakes. Before deciding how to mark individual students' written work teachers new to a school would be well advised to find out about the school's marking policy. On the one hand it can be argued that, for some students, repeatedly receiving back scripts covered with marks indicating errors is very demoralising. On the other, there has to be a rational, structured approach to ensure that students make progress in recognising mistakes and learning how to correct them. Teachers may feel it is appropriate to encourage students to proof read their own, or peers', work before handing it in, and/or, perhaps, to correct only words or sentence structure with which they feel students should already be familiar.

SUMMARY

As practitioners, teachers need to bear in mind factors related to the individual child, to the condition (if one has been identified) associated with that child the wider cultural and social factors, the curriculum and also the school context. The view that failure to learn can result from social and arrangements that fail to support students' engagement with their learning as much as from attributes of individuals (Lave, 1993, p. 10) can lead to a very positive approach to overcome the difficulties that are experienced. It has the advantage of giving teachers and students more control over learning in that appropriate attention to these areas can lead to improved student learning. Also teachers can have confidence that students will acquire learn and make progress if appropriate strategies are devised to address their difficulties and facilitate children's increasing participation in school.

5

UNDERSTANDING AND ADDRESSING DIFFICULTIES IN BEHAVIOUR, EMOTIONAL AND SOCIAL DEVELOPMENT

INTRODUCTION

This chapter focuses on difficulties experienced by children and young people who demonstrate features of emotional and behavioural difficulties (EBD). Special attention will be given to young people's behaviour experienced by teachers and others as extremely challenging, including attention deficit/hyperactivity disorder (AD/HD), physical violence and bullying, and withdrawn behaviour associated with trauma such as bereavement and emotional deprivation. The aim will be to illustrate

- what research tells us about these difficulties: causal factors and common indicators,
- the relationship between the experience of social and emotional difficulties and learning,
- ways that the barriers to learning experienced by young people with these difficulties can be addressed in school and elsewhere.

Interpretations of, and responses to, behaviour perceived as challenging at home and/or in schools often generate a great deal of heated debate. Schools play a critical part in shaping a child's identity as a learner (Bruner, 1996). This chapter takes as its main frame of reference for understanding pupil behaviour that the human mind actively constructs its own reality and makes its own sense of every situation and context. Young people's behaviour must therefore relate to the way that they make sense of their worlds. Rejecting schooling is nearly always a strongly emotional experience (Furlong, 1985). For this reason, careful account needs to be taken of students' own sense-making, even if this may be experienced as uncomfortable at times. The chapter also takes the view that:

- belonging is a fundamental human need, as Maslow's hierarchy (1943), for example, clearly indicates;
- teachers and families can put themselves into a much stronger position to deal with problematic behaviour by recognising that the way students behave may be explained by factors within classrooms and within schools as well as factors associated with those students (Wearmouth *et al.*, 2004);
- student behaviour occurs in interaction between the learning environment and the individual. Addressing difficult student behaviour effectively must relate to the way that students make sense of their own worlds as well to consideration of the learning environment in which that behaviour occurs (ibid.).

FRAMES OF REFERENCE IN THE AREA OF BEHAVIOUR DIFFICULTIES

Schooling is an integral part of society, not simply a way of preparing for entry to that society (Bruner, 1996). 'Difficult' neighbourhoods tend to produce more 'difficult' students than neighbourhoods in more affluent circumstances (Watkins and Wagner, 2000). However, economic impoverishment in the neighbourhood does not necessarily lead to disruptive behaviour in schools (Rutter *et al.*, 1979, OFSTED, 2001). Even in areas of disadvantage, good classroom management as well as interventions with individual students, can make a difference to student behaviour, learning and future life chances.

The frames of reference for understanding problematic behaviour really matter. In schools this can have a strong effect on the way teachers deal with students and their parents or carers. We might take the example of 'Maladjusted Jack' and consider how different interpretations of his behaviour might lead to different kinds of intervention:

THE EXAMPLE OF 'MALADJUSTED JACK'

'Maladjusted Jack' was a participant in a series of interviews with adult male inmates in one of Her Majesty's (HM) prisons (Wearmouth, 1999). He gives an account of how he was born into an unsettled family and was taken into care at any early age as a result of his parents' divorce and his sister's inability to provide for him adequately:

> My parents split up when I was three and I went to live with my sister. She already had two children of her own, and she couldn't cope with me as well. She put me into care.

Social Services were involved in his life from an early stage. When he started infant school he was deemed to be out of control because he used to run around, disrupt classrooms, upset the dustbins in the school yard and climb on to the roof. He was quickly referred to an educational psychologist for an assessment of his behaviour.

NURTURING YOUNG CHILDREN IN SCHOOLS

One psychological theory of human development that has had considerable influence over educational provision for young children like Jack whose behaviour is of concern to teachers is that of attachment theory (Bowlby, 1952). As Holmes (1993, p. 39) notes, implicit in this theory is the view that:

> children deprived of maternal care ... may be seriously affected in their physical, intellectual, emotional and social development ... prolonged separation of a child from his mother (or mother substitute) during the first five years of life stands foremost among the causes of delinquent character development.
>
> (Bowlby, 1944, 1952)

Babies quickly attach themselves emotionally to their adult carers and progress through well-recognized stages of development towards maturity. Successful development depends on needs being adequately met at an earlier stage. Where this is not the case, then children will persist in inappropriate attachment behaviour, being over-anxious, avoidant or aggressive, or becoming incapable of warm attachment and positive human relationships (Harris-Hendriks and Figueroa, 1995; Bennathan, 2000).

Attachment theory has influenced education in the early years through the development of 'nurture groups' in some infant schools, originally in the Inner London Education Authority in 1970–1971 by Marjorie Boxall, an educational psychologist, and re-established more recently by some local authorities. Boxall (2002) argues that learning, personality and behaviour difficulties, which are more likely in the young children of families experiencing disadvantage and deprivation, can be the result of inadequate early care and support from parents who struggle with poverty, damaged relationships and harsh and stressful living conditions. The underlying assumption of the nurture group is that children such as Jack who have fared badly though the learning processes of early childhood need extra support and appropriate experiences. This means recreating in school the total experience of a normally developing child from babyhood onwards and planning the routine of the nurture group day to provide a predictable, reliable structure in which children can go on to interact and learn in regular settings (Bennathan, 2000).

FEATURES OF NURTURE GROUPS

The nurture group attempts to create the features of adequate parenting within school with opportunities to develop trust, security, positive mood and identity through attachment to a reliable attentive and caring adult, as well as autonomy through the provision of controlled and graduated experiences in familiar surroundings. Some features of such groups include: easy physical contact between adult and child; warmth, intimacy and a family atmosphere; good-humoured acceptance of children and their behaviour; familiar regular routines; a focus on tidying up and putting away; the provision of food in structured contexts; opportunities to play and the appropriate participation of the adults; adults talking about, and encouraging reflection by children on, trouble-provoking situations and their own feelings; opportunities for children to develop increasing autonomy. These opportunities incorporate visits outside the nurture group, participation

> in games, visits to regular classrooms and children's eventual full-time inclusion in a mainstream class.
>
> (Wearmouth, 2009, p. 167)

Bennathan (2000) comments that nurture groups accept and work with children with serious social behaviour developmental difficulties who present major challenges to regular class teachers and other students so that they can be included in mainstream schooling. If Jack had been included in a nurture group, the critical challenge would have been to ensure that the group role remained a short-term developmental one and that Jack would be included in regular classrooms after a relatively short time.

Nurture groups had only been established in Inner London when Jack was young, however, not in his home area. The psychologist to whom he was referred assessed him as 'maladjusted', and Social Services and the local education authority decided to send him away to a boarding school for 'maladjusted' pupils at the age of six. Thus began his career in special schools, first through his primary years and then through secondary.

Examination of the rise and demise of this category is an interesting example of the way in which the use of labels attaching problems to children can pervade the education system to suit the existing national context.

THE CASE OF 'MALADJUSTMENT' (ADAPTED FROM WEARMOUTH, 2009, p. 21)

Before 1945 there was no formal category of 'maladjustment' included in Ministry of Education regulations. It had its origins in the establishment of a group of children identified as moral imbeciles or defectives under the terms of the 1913 Act. Children who showed emotionally disturbed or disruptive behaviour came to be associated with both mental defect and moral defect (Galloway *et al.*, 1994, p. 110). Board of Education Reports in the 1920s, for example, identified 'unstable', 'nervous', 'difficult and maladjusted' children as in need of child guidance (ibid., p. 112).

After 1945 all LEAs had a responsibility to establish special educational treatment in special or ordinary schools for students defined as 'maladjusted'. The concept was still relatively new when the Underwood Committee was set-up in 1950 to enquire into 'maladjusted' students' medical, educational and social problems. The Underwood Report (1955, Chapter IV, para. 96) lists six symptoms of 'maladjustment' requiring professional help from psychologists, child guidance clinics or doctors: 'nervous disorders', for example fears, depression, apathy and excitability; 'habit disorders', for example speech defects, sleep-walking, twitching and incontinence; 'behaviour disorders', for example defiance, aggression, jealousy and stealing; 'organic disorders', for example cerebral tumours, psychotic behaviour; for example delusions, bizarre behaviour, and 'educational and vocational difficulties'; for example inability to concentrate or keep jobs.

An overall definition proved difficult. There has never been a consensus on what defines 'problem behaviour', of the sort categorised by the term 'maladjusted'. As Galloway (1987, p. 32) comments: ' ... the common point to emerge from attempts to clarify behavioural disorders and types of maladjustment is that it is a ragbag term describing any kind of behaviour that teachers and parents find disturbing'.

Invent the category, create the pupil! 'Maladjustment' was often used pragmatically to justify special educational provision for those students for whom segregation from peers has been seen as necessary. Invent the category, create the student. Between 1945–1960, the numbers of students classified as maladjusted rose from 0 to 1742. 'Psychiatrists have sometimes been prone to see pathology in all kinds of variations of personality and styles of life' (Rutter *et al.*, 1970, p. 178).

In 1970, Rutter *et al.* attempted to assess the prevalence of specific categories of difficulties in the school student population. Estimates of maladjustment in the child population varied across the country from 5 to 25 per cent. Furlong (1985) notes that, by 1975, there were 13,000 students labelled as 'maladjusted'. Ravenette's (1984, p. 4) identification of three situations where the word 'maladjustment' was commonly used shows clearly how the maladjusted descriptor was used to explain Jack's behaviour:

1. There is a breakdown in the relationship between a child and others which is chronic rather than transitory.
2. The adults in the situation are worried by the behaviour which points to a breakdown and by their inability to do anything about it.

> 3. It is then a signal to others that the situation is intolerable, that the institution is entitled to some special help or relief and that perhaps the child should be placed in a more appropriate institution, or be rendered 'normal' by treatment.

These days Jack would not be identified as maladjusted because the term no longer exists as a formal descriptor of student behaviour in schools. 'Maladjusted' has been replaced by descriptors such as EBD, or 'social, emotional and behavioural difficulties' (SEBD) which still enable removal of students from mainstream on occasions.

EMOTIONAL AND BEHAVIOURAL DIFFICULTIES

The frame of reference relating to the terms EBD, first formally used by Warnock (1978), or SEBD, are just as ill-defined as that relating to maladjustment. Use of this term to explain why some students behave badly or inappropriately is not always helpful to parents and/or teachers. Poulou and Norwich (2002, p. 112), for example, found from a review of international studies that it can influence teachers' confidence in their abilities to respond to students' needs in classrooms and ' … can generate feelings of helplessness and incompetence' (Lennox, 1991; Bennett, 1992; Leadbetter and Leadbetter, 1993; Chazan *et al.*, 1994; Gray *et al.*, 1996)'. The more teachers thought student behaviour stemmed from problems within the students themselves, such as the 'child wants to attract attention' or the 'child's innate personality', ' … the more they experienced feelings of "stress", "offence" and even "helplessness", especially for conduct and mixed behaviour difficulties' (Poulou and Norwich, 2002, p. 125).

Young people's behaviour does not occur in a vacuum (Watkins and Wagner, 2000). Teachers see themselves as able to deal with a student's problematic behaviour if they consider that students' problems generally are caused by 'factors originating from teachers themselves, like their personality, manners towards the child with EBD, or teaching style' (ibid.). In other words, if they think they can control the cause of a difficulty they believe 'that they can also sufficiently treat it. In addition, they perceived themselves in such cases as even more responsible for finding an effective solution for the child's problem' (Poulou and Norwich, 2002, p. 112).

As already discussed in Chapter 2, most commonly, understandings and strategies in classroom management are based on principles from a behaviourist psychology frame of reference (Skinner, 1938; Baer *et al.*, 1968). Behavioural methodologies hold that all (mis)behaviour is learned and, therefore, that learning and (mis)behaviour can be modified through intervening in a systematic, consistent, predictable way in the environment. Classroom and school rules are examples of antecedent conditions (or setting events) that are intended to signify behaviour that is acceptable or appropriate. Such rules can also provide punishing consequences for behaviour that is unacceptable.

TEN PRINCIPLES FOR CONTROLLING AND MODIFYING BEHAVIOUR

Ten principles for controlling and modifying students' behaviour in schools are summarised below from Berryman and Glynn (2001). The first four aim to manage behaviour through attending to the antecedent conditions, that is aspects of the context, that precede or accompany it. The other six principles aim to modify unwanted behaviours through changing the contingencies of reinforcement, that is the rewards or punishment, that follow it.

Changing behaviour by altering the antecedents of the behaviour:

1. Careful planning ahead to foresee possible behaviour difficulties that are likely to arise, and preparing strategies and responses ahead of time, can help to avoid challenging or undesirable behaviours.
2. Altering aspects of the context in which undesirable behaviour occurs can influence that behaviour. For example, ensuring that classroom equipment is properly organised and available and rearranging desks and chairs, can make a difference.
3. Give clear instructions that are polite, clear and concise as an antecedent condition for compliant behaviour. Before an instruction is given, gain the child's or student's full attention to avoid unnecessary repeating of instructions which can undermine their effectiveness.
4. Model the behaviour that is wanted, that is specific ways of behaving in particular situations. Pupils then may imitate that

behaviour in similar situations. Students may imitate negative as well as positive behaviour however, for example abusive or sarcastic language. Modelling may have even stronger effects if the observer sees the modeller being rewarded (Bandura, 1969).

Changing behaviours by altering the contingencies of reinforcement:

5. Provide positive predictable consequences. Behaviour learnt most readily is that which consistently has positive consequences. This can include social attention, praise, recognition, access to favourite activities, and so on.

6. Intervene at an early stage. The earlier the intervention to check undesirable behaviour, the easier it is to prevent behaviour from escalating into a major problem.

7. Accept gradual improvement. It is important to provide positive consequences for quite small changes in behaviour to begin with.

8. A little and often. The frequencies of opportunities students have to experience the consequences of their behaviour is important.

9. Define and select another behaviour the student can perform that is incompatible with the undesirable or unacceptable behaviour, and reinforce this with positive consequences.

10. Clearly define sanctions, explain them to children, and very carefully implement them for a specified length of time. Implementing these sanctions should not either model or provoke further physical or verbal abuse and should never be accompanied by emotional or angry 'put down' and abusive comments. Sanctions should be removed when specific behaviour change criteria have been met.

The boarding primary school that Maladjusted Jack was sent to appears from his description to have been run along strict behaviourist lines. He appears to have thrived in a context where he could see purpose in what he was expected to do, and where discipline was strict but very fair. He recalled with respect a particular teacher who

… wasn't too bad a bloke really. He was very fair – very strict, though. He played a game called Leggo because if you misbehaved you got a slap across the legs with this metre ruler and you went: 'Oh, that hurt!' That's why we called it Leggo.

He remembered with affection a woman teacher who used social reinforcers of praise and extra attention to reinforce behaviour that she saw as acceptable and desirable:

Mrs F. She was probably my best teacher ever. She really did try and help me a lot. She took me under her wing. She saw the potential in me, and tried to bring out the best in me. She was very motherly to me – she stuck up for me when no one else would.

Lack of structure and disorganisation in the secondary special school for maladjusted pupils to which he was transferred, however, led very predictably to frustration, rage and very uncontrolled behaviour:

The school was total crap. It was rubbish. It was totally unorganised. There was no foresight in the school at all. There was no purpose. I wasn't studying towards exams, I was going over the same things again. The things they tried to teach me, I'd already done it.... I was laughing in their face because I knew how far they could push, how far they can go. I've been in children's homes and in boarding schools, so I know exactly how far they can go with you. When they overstepped the mark I was the first one to step in there and say: 'You can't do that!'

Finally he was sent to a secure psychiatric unit:

I was in there for seven months. 'Beyond control', they actually said. I was locked up, wasn't I? It was just another institution where you had to learn to run the rules and bend them to your best advantage ... I was totally out of it. I thought: 'You've ruined my education, now you watch me, putting you through it, putting you through the grinding mill'.... I was out to beat them any way I could do.

(Wearmouth, 1997)

BEREAVEMENT IN CHILDHOOD

One of the events in childhood that is likely to affect children's behaviour very profoundly, and, indeed, may have resonances later on in life, is that of the death of the primary caregiver, most often the mother, or of close family members. According to CRUSE (2010), one in 29 children aged 5–16 in the United Kingdom has been bereaved of a parent or sibling, and one in 16 has lost a close friend (http://www.thebighug.org.uk/). The deep distress that results from a child's bereavement may create a special educational need of a short- or long-term nature.

Children need a secure, affectionate and continuous experience of care from a small number of caregivers in order to grow into emotionally secure and sociable adults. When children are born there follows a period of developing mutual attachment between child and caregiver. The pattern of attachment that is established between the child and primary caregiver is a source of security that remains important throughout life. Black (1998) notes that: 'Infant attachment is at its height at about 3 years of age and then becomes increasingly diffused by the development of other relationships, but it remains important throughout life, with later relationships qualitatively echoing the other ones' (p. 931).

Infants' and toddlers' reactions to long term or permanent separation from an attachment figure generally follow a predictable pattern. Crying, searching restlessly and high anxiety are followed by a period of despair and, eventually 'pathological states of detachment and indifference may ensue' (ibid.). Children who have lost one caregiver often become very anxious about the safety of others. They may also have feeding and sleeping difficulties.

PERSONAL REFLECTIONS ON SEPARATION FROM A PARENT

My mother was taken into hospital for a long period of about three months when I was 4 years old. I couldn't eat or sleep and became very thin. I was sent to stay with an aunt, and I can remember being distraught when she went out anywhere without me. I didn't realise why, at the time. I had never been particularly close to her.

(Wearmouth, unpublished)

Some people may assume that a young person who loses a parent, caregiver, sibling or grandparent will not be affected too deeply as she/he is too young and emotional disturbances may last for several years (Rutter, 1966). Weller *et al.* (1991), for example, found that over one-third of their sample of bereaved children had serious depressive reactions a year after bereavement. CRUSE (2010) comments that it is common for 'some bereaved children and young people to delay their grief for months or sometimes years'. Subsequently, 'other life changing incidents such as moving home, acquiring a step parent or experiencing a further bereavement can serve to release the bereaved child or young person's delayed or unresolved grief.' There seems to be no way to divert grief. '. . . ultimately, regardless of how long the child or young person has managed to deny their grief, they will have to go through the grieving process eventually' (ibid., http://www.crusebereavementcare.org.uk/SchoolsChanges.html).

Commonly children and adolescents long to be reunited with the dead parent and may experience suicidal thoughts. When the death is of the mother, the quality of the care given to the child may also be reduced (Black, 1998). When the death in the family is of a sibling, the child may feel guilty at having survived when the brother or sister has died. The child may also believe that she/he is to blame in some way for the death. This may lead to profound changes in the child's behaviour (ibid.).

SUPPORT FOR BEREAVED CHILDREN

Studies of grief among bereaved adults indicate that the process and period of mourning is assisted if children are told in advance that the parent is likely to die (Parkes, 1986). Children who know beforehand experience lower levels of anxiety than those who do not (Rosenheim and Reicher, 1985).

CHILDREN NEED TO GRIEVE, TOO

Children need to be allowed to attend the funeral as part of the grieving process, but should be protected from the raw grief that may be expressed (Black, 1998).

> I was 9 when my mother died. My dad didn't let my sister and me go to the funeral. I guess it was because he couldn't cope

> himself. I was 32 before I found out where my mum's grave was. When I first saw it, it was like she had died just yesterday. The grief was overwhelming.
>
> (Wearmouth, unpublished)

Long-term support for practical aspects of child care is clearly very important for the welfare of the bereaved child. Family therapy that focuses on sharing the experience of loss and grief in the family and supports talking about the dead parent of caregiver can help the grieving process (Black and Urbanowicz, 1987; Weller *et al.*, 1991).

As Cruse (2010a, 2010b) notes, above all, young people need to be given the opportunity to grieve. Ignoring or averting the child's grief is not supportive, but can prove extremely damaging as the child becomes an adult. Young people need to be allowed to talk about their feelings. Everyone has their own way of grieving. Not all young people will experience the same emotions, behave the same way respond similarly to other people who have lost close friends or relations.

MEDICAL AND BIOLOGICAL EXPLANATIONS OF BEHAVIOUR

In the context of school, the differences in world views held by different professional groups and their different ways of working may have a very important influence over students' educational experiences in schools. Medical and biological explanations of behaviour theorise problems as inherent to an individual. From a medical or biological view, behaviour experienced by others as difficult or challenging is the result of an underlying condition, disease or dysfunction which an individual has and which requires treatment.

ATTENTION DEFICIT/HYPERACTIVITY DISORDER

One of the conditions that is sometimes attributed to a biological cause is attention deficit/hyperactivity disorder (AD/HD). AD/HD is described by Norwich *et al.* (2002, p. 182) as 'a medical diagnosis of the American Psychiatric Association' that is

> characterised by chronic and pervasive (to home and school) problems of inattention, impulsiveness, and/or excessive motor activity which have seriously debilitating effects on individuals' social, emotional and educational development, and are sometimes disruptive to the home and/or school environment.

According to the British Psychological Society (1996), between 2 and 5 per cent of British school students are believed to experience this condition. There are interesting differences in the reported incidence of AD/HD internationally which are explained by some researchers as related to prevailing variations in cultural practices. There is a strict requirement for 'pervasiveness and persistence' across a range of contexts. This means that behaviour which is seen largely in one context only does not constitute grounds for a diagnosis.

Defining AD/HD as a mental disorder is problematic. 'We have evidence that children given the diagnosis AD/HD don't attend, don't wait and don't sit still. But just because they don't do all these things does not mean that they cannot do them' (BPS, 1996, p. 23).

As the AD/HD Association of New Zealand suggests, while no one really knows what causes AD/HD, the general consensus among the medical and scientific community is that AD/HD is biological in nature. Many believe that it results from a chemical imbalance in the brain.

In some cases, a medical diagnosis of the cause of challenging or inappropriate behaviour in schools results in a prescription for particular kinds of medication. The use of psychostimulants is based on a theory of biochemical imbalance.

> The medication stimulates areas of the brain regulating arousal and alertness and can result in immediate short-term improvements in concentration and impulse control. The precise mechanism is poorly understood and the specific locus of action within the central nervous system remains speculative.
>
> (Ibid., pp. 50–1)

Some researchers suspect that stimulants work through the release of neurotransmitters, powerful chemical messengers. Neurons in the brain do not actually connect to each other. There is a gap between them. Neurons communicate through neurotransmitters that are passed between them. Many researchers have suspected that AD/HD may result from problems related to communication between neurons. Of the most commonly used stimulants, methylphenidate (Ritalin) is most widely prescribed. It is usually administered in the form of tablets to be taken at regularly.

One major concern about the use of such psychostimulants relates to the effects and side effects of these drugs. There is also an ethical issue concerning the lack of adequate monitoring of the day to day classroom learning and behavioural outcomes of medication prescribed for many students.

> [E]ducational practitioners are concerned about the so-called 'zombie' effect (Sharron, 1995) which may be the result of inappropriate doses and poor monitoring. There is also evidence of 'behavioural rebound' in the afternoons when the medication wears off. These concerns illustrate the practical issues of managing medication at home and at school [as well as the ethical risks in relying on medication alone, without providing appropriate learning tasks and activities that attract positive reinforcement, to bring about behaviour change at school].
>
> (Ibid., pp. 51–2)

Although the prescription of a chemical psychostimulant is fairly common, as noted by the British Psychological Society (1996), apart from all the ethical considerations, prescribing a drug provides an insufficient response. 'Medication must not become the first, and definitely not the only, line of treatment' (BPS, 1996, p. 2). Also needed are appropriate social support mechanisms in school and outside, including ways to address barriers to learning within the classroom or school context. Focusing on the medical and/or biological bases alone to explain behaviour is likely to provide an insufficient remedy because it ignores the holistic nature of well-being and, therefore, all those other elements which contribute to it. Students' core values associated with self-identity, self-esteem and a sense of purpose as a functioning member of a social and cultural group must also be considered in addressing overall well-being. There is a great deal of room for exploring ways in which more inclusive pedagogies within classrooms and schools might improve the learning and behaviour of students who are diagnosed as AD/HD.

The use of psychostimulants is not the only common response to the issue of behaviour related to AD/HD. In a summary of 150 intervention studies of students with AD/HD, (BPS, 1996, pp. 47–8) seven approaches are identified which are based on a cognitive–behavioural viewpoint. These approaches focus on the effects of consequences through positive reinforcement, response cost and training in the reduction of behaviour viewed as problematic. Positive reinforcement or token reinforcement can result in reduced activity, increased 'time on task' and improved academic performance. 'Several studies showed that behaviour management and medication were most effective when combined'. Mildly aversive procedures (reprimands or redirection) can be effective with Primary age children, especially when combined with positive reinforcement. A combination of positive and negative reinforcement procedures and 'response cost' that is mild punishment designed to make the undesirable, behaviour more difficult and more of an effort to perform has also been successful in some studies. Biofeedback involving providing the child with some form of visual or auditory feedback on levels of physiological states (e.g. heart rate) with a view to the child learning to control and monitor those states has also had some measure of success.

There is also some evidence that a few students experience intolerance to particular foods and there is the suggestion of a link between this and difficult behaviour. 'Common allergens included additives, chocolate, dairy products, wheat, oranges and other fruit. These particular substances are found in many commercially produced foods and medicines' (BPS, 1996, p. 52). The area of the influence of diet over behaviour is largely under-researched and controversial.

THE ISSUE OF PHYSICAL RESTRAINT

Whatever label might be given to difficult behaviour, dealing with severe behaviour incidents is far more challenging and stressful for a teacher or others than dealing with mildly disruptive incidents. However, an appropriate response is often the same. On occasions, students may be aggressive, out of control and a danger to themselves and others. It is very important to minimise the risk of physical confrontation in the first instance, rather than having to take action after the event. It seems sensible for teachers to avoid confrontations with students where these can be avoided. However, many of us have experienced situations when they cannot be, for instance, if asked by a colleague to help in some crisis, or where a student's provocative behaviour may have become intolerable. Dunckley (1999) refers to physical restraint as a last resort that should only be used to manage a dangerous situation. It should be employed carefully and in accordance with school policies, that should indicate when restraint can be used. It may be necessary to remove a student from a group of peers. This can be achieved 'by asking the other students to leave. It may be more appropriate, and safer, to bring other staff to the place where the student is, rather than the other way around' (ibid., p. 10). It is important for those associated with schools to check school, local area and/ or national policies on physical restraint of students in schools.

There are a number of important ethical issues surrounding the restraint of students against their will (Bowers, 1996; Cooper, 1999; Cornwall, 2000). There is a difference between physical restraint, to hold a student still until aggression (hitting, kicking and punching others) subsides, and punitive incarcerations such as locking the student away for extended periods of time, as can occur when the principles of 'time out' are misunderstood, or misapplied, often in the heat of the moment (Cornwall, 2004). Dunckley (1999, p. 16) comments that students who are 'in an agitated state' need 'guidance and direction to increase their sense of security ... where possible and appropriate give a choice, time for the student to respond, then, after an appropriate time, follow through with consequences'.

TOURETTE SYNDROME

Tourette syndrome (TS) is a neurological disorder characterised by motor and vocal tics: repetitive, stereotyped, involuntary movements and vocalisations. As National Institute of Neorological Disorders and Stroke [(NINDS) 2005] outlines, motor tics are, commonly, sudden, brief, repetitive movements that may include eye blinking and other vision irregularities, facial grimacing, shoulder shrugging and head or shoulder jerking, or, more dramatically, touching objects, hopping, jumping, bending, twisting or motor movements that result in self-harm such as punching oneself in the face. Vocalisations often include repetitive throat-clearing, sniffing or grunting sounds – or, at the extreme, 'coprolalia' (uttering swear words) or 'echolalia' (repeating the words or phrases of others). People with TS often report that tics are preceded by an urge or sensation in the affected muscles, commonly called a 'premonitory urge' that builds up to the point where it is expressed. Excitement, anxiety or particular physical experiences can trigger or worsen tics.

Across the world the prevalence among school children 'range from 1 to 10 per 1,000, with a rate of 6 per 1,000 replicated in several countries' (Piacenti *et al.*, 2010, p. 1929). Evidence from twin and family studies suggests that TS may be genetic (NINDS, 2005). Tics tend to start in early childhood, peak before the mid-teen years and improve subsequently. Approximately 10 per cent of young people have symptoms that last into adulthood. Medication can be prescribed for young people whose tics are severe enough to interfere with their functioning. The most effective appear to be antipsychotics. However, as Piacenti *et al.* (2010, p. 1930) comment, these 'rarely eliminate tics and are often associated with unacceptable sedation, weight gain, cognitive dulling, and motor adverse effects', such as tremors.

In recent years particular interventions based on a behaviourist approach have been developed that seem, from small controlled trials, to be effective in reducing tic severity (NINDS, 2005). For example, 'habit reversal training' acknowledges that tics have a neurological basis and also, in its design, takes into account the context in which the individual lives and works as well as the internal experience of premonitory urges. Piacenti *et al.* (2010, p. 1930) describe the main components of habit reversal as tic-awareness and 'competing-response training'. Awareness training comprises self-monitoring of tics and the early signs that a tic is about to occur. Competing-response training involves deliberately engaging in a behaviour that is not physically compatible with the tic as soon as the premonitory urge is felt. In this way tics are not suppressed. Instead, the individual is taught to manage the urge and initiate an alternative socially acceptable behaviour that replaces the tic. The competing response can be initiated when the patient notices that a tic is about to occur, during the tic or after the tic has occurred. For vocal tics, the most commonly competing response that is taught is slow rhythmic breathing from the diaphragm. With practice, patients are able to complete the competing response without disengaging from routine activities.

Young people with TS often cope well in mainstream classrooms. However, frequent tics can interfere with academic performance or disrupt social relationships with peers. My own experience is that, in a well-managed classroom, other young people can be very understanding and supportive. All young people with TS, as with any other kind of special educational need, benefit from a learning environment that is supportive and flexible enough to accommodate their individual learning needs. This may mean making special arrangements if the tics disrupt the pupil's ability to write, or problem solving with the pupil on ways to reduce stress in the classroom or during examinations.

BULLYING BEHAVIOUR

An example of student behaviour which is the focus of teachers' concerns in many schools and which can be explained from a variety of viewpoints is that of bullying. Rigby (2002) concludes that, from his analysis of work on what constitutes bullying behaviour (e.g. Randall, 1991; Farrington, 1993; Olweus, 1993, 1999; Smith and Sharp, 1994), bullying is a combination of the wish to hurt somebody together with hurtful action, an imbalance and unjust use of power, enjoyment on the part of the bully, the victim's feeling of oppression and, often, repetition of the bullying behaviour.

THE INFLUENCE OF SITUATIONAL FACTORS ON BULLYING BEHAVIOUR

The Second World War and then, later, the war in Vietnam, stimulated interest in a clear focus within social psychology research projects into the issues of obedience to malign authority, and the influence of group pressure to conform to a group norm where the actions of one person or a group acting under the orders of an authoritative other were clearly to the detriment of another. For example, Milgram's (1963, 1974) 'electric shock' experiments were designed to investigate the extent to which individuals were prepared to obey authoritative instructions from others to deliver electric shocks to adult learners.

Studies on conformity and obedience typically indicate a 'fundamental attribution error' (Nisbett *et al.* 1973); that is, that people generally overestimate the role of the characteristics of individual people and underestimate the role of contextual factors in regulating human behaviour (Atkinson *et al.*, 1993). Zimbardo's (1970) 'prison experiment' where volunteers acting the part of prison guards were prepared to humiliate and victimise other volunteers acting as 'prisoners' is an example of the kind of experiment designed to test the hypothesis that, under certain conditions, members of a group can lose their personal identities and experience a sense of mob aggression and much greater impulsive behaviour against other individuals.

Contemporary studies of bullying in schools in various countries indicate that the incidence of bullying by peers appears to be more common in some countries than others (Rigby, 2002). Within countries Rigby (1997) has shown that differences between schools in the incidence of bullying can also be considerable. It is noteworthy that, in schools, there is a negative relationship between the presence of teachers at break times and lunchtimes and bullying (Olweus, 1993).

THE CYCLE OF BULLYING

Bullying is often associated with an imbalance of power between victim and perpetrator. Once the victim begins to react to the bullying by showing signs of stress, the bully or bullies may experience great pleasure and enjoyment from their feelings of power and dominance. The cycle of bullying may continue and/or grow more intense and continue for a long time. Sometimes the victim may fight back (literally), sometimes she/he may find ways to avoid the bullying by hovering around teachers or staying at home.

One of the crucial factors in accounting for the degree of severity of bullying in schools is the behaviour of bystanders. Research on bystander behaviour assumed popularity after a murder of the New Yorker, Kitty Genovese, in 1964, which became notorious as a result of the non-intervention of 38 neighbours who heard her screams for help for over 30 minutes but failed to assist her (Atkinson *et al.*, 1993). Social psychologists researching what they termed 'bystander apathy' found that the presence of others seems to deter individuals from intervening in difficult or dangerous situations where they could be of assistance to the person in danger or trouble. However, a training programme focusing on raising awareness of bystander apathy can be shown to make a significant difference to the preparedness of bystanders to help others in trouble (Beaman *et al.*, 1978). The abduction in England of a young boy, James Bulger, was also witnessed by many bystanders who did nothing to intervene with the 10-year-olds who marched him around Liverpool before murdering him. Another factor which appears to be of consequence in inhibiting intervention is the perceived relationship between these boys. They were assumed to be brothers (Levine, 1999).

Group pressure to conform to a majority view can also be shown to influence individuals to act against their own judgements. In a classic series of studies, Asch (1952, 1955, 1958) showed that individuals confronted with the unanimous views of a group about an issue were unlikely to disagree openly with the group's judgement even when this was clearly wrong. In Asch's experiments individuals were asked to judge the length of a line that was clearly estimated incorrectly by the group. Many subjects preferred to accede to the group's view rather than risk challenging the group's apparent competence and thus the fear of 'What will they think of me?' (Atkinson *et al.*, 1993).

Rigby (2002) warns against any assumption that the descriptors 'bully' and 'victim' should suggest a stable personality trait. Many of those who bully in their younger years do not repeat this behaviour later on. Some of those who bully in one situation would never do so in another.

It is tempting to think of bullies as being socially inadequate (Field, 1999). However, this may be a gross oversimplification. To take advantage of, and manipulate, other less powerful individuals, bullies may need to be very skilful in the social situation (Sutton *et al.*, 1999). On measures of self-esteem school bullies are average (Rigby, 1997). However, bullies tend to be less able to imagine another's point of view (Rigby, 2002) and to experience stronger feelings of depression (Slee, 1995). They also appear to be more positively disposed towards violence (Olweus, 1993).

Despite the risk of supporting the use of stereotypes, there does seem to be some consensus among researchers about the correlates of victimisation. For example, victims of bullying may have low self-worth and self-esteem, be non-assertive and have poor social skills, be introverted, relatively uncooperative and physically less strong than others. They may also be physically shorter than others, be lonely and isolated, and prone to anxiety, depression and suicide (Rigby, 2002, pp. 139–40).

Responses to bullying behaviour in schools often fall into one of the two categories. There are those that assume bullying is an antisocial act which needs to be reduced through the application of responses from a behaviourist approach, such as various types of punishment contingencies. From this view 'we can best proceed by identifying and punishing behaviour we wish to stop' (ibid., p. 463). Typically any violation of rules is treated similarly whether major or minor. Policies may rely completely on 'rules and sanctions and zero tolerance for rule infractions' (ibid., p. 238). Other responses focus on establishing respectful behaviour between people so as to minimise bullying through the abuse of power in personal relationships (Rigby, 2002). From this view, 'positive improvement in behaviour between people can be brought about through instruction, persuasion and modelling of respectful behaviour' (ibid., p. 238).

'CIRCLE TIME'

One initiative associated with the resolution of students' disputes at primary school level in schools in the United Kingdom that depends on listening to the views of the student community in classrooms is that of 'Circle Time' (Mosley, 1996). As Tew (1998, p. 20) comments, in many traditional communities the circle is a symbol of 'unity, healing and power' and can be found in the traditions of groups as diverse 'as the North American Indians and Anglo Saxon monks'. Wearmouth *et al.* (2004) note that, in schools, 'Circle Time' is a meeting that follows strict protocols of involving all participants in discussion where both teachers and students are bound by rules that stipulate no one may put anyone down, no one may use any name negatively (creating 'safety' for all individuals including teachers and parents) and when individuals speak, everyone must listen.

Everyone has a turn and a chance to speak, all views are taken seriously, members of the class team suggest ways of solving problems and individuals can accept the help or politely refuse it (Wearmouth *et al.*, 2005, p. 184).

The rules must be followed strictly. If a student breaks a rule a visual warning is given. If this persists, time away from the circle follows.

RESTORATIVE PRACTICE

In some schools and local areas, particular programmes have been designed to focus on traditional community values in order to harness the necessary resources to address problems that have resulted in, and as a result of, unacceptable, unsociable behaviours (Schweigert, 1999). One such initiative is based in general terms on the principles of 'restorative justice'. The prime focus in a restorative justice approach is on 'putting things right' between all those involved or affected by wrongdoing. Restorative justice can employ traditional conflict resolution processes and culturally appropriate mechanisms drawn from the external community to address and resolve tension and make justice visible and more productive in communities inside the school (Anderson *et al.*, 1996). In New Zealand, for example, where restorative justice practices are influenced by traditional Maori cultural values and preferred ways of responding to wrongdoing, the emphasis is on the restoration of harmony between the individual, the victim and the collective (tribe or sub-tribe). In order for restoration to take place, all those involved in the offence 'need to be heard in the process of seeking redress' (Restorative Practices Development Team, 2003, p. 11).

AN EXAMPLE OF A RESTORATIVE APPROACH

Wearmouth *et al.* (2007) describe an example of restorative practice where the teachers, mother and wider family members of 15-year-old 'Wiremu' had become increasingly concerned about his negative, challenging behaviour in school and antisocial activities outside.

Things came to a head when he took his mother's car out joyriding and crashed into the neighbour's garden, damaging the gnomes given to the elderly neighbour by his deceased wife. The behaviour support teacher to whom he had been referred organised a meeting at the local rugby club where Wiremu was a keen member, and invited everyone who knew him to attend. When the boy arrived, unaware of the true reason why he was being taken to the club, everyone was given a chance to speak about him, teachers, community elders, friends and relations. Mostly it was in very glowing terms – about his captaincy of a rugby team, his personal qualities, and so on. Then his mother talked about the loss of the car that meant so much to the family, and the neighbour talked about his dead wife and the broken gnomes.

> What happened next had surprised everybody. Wiremu stood up to speak. He was crying. He turned to the elderly neighbour whose garden he had wrecked and asked to be forgiven. He offered to help mend the fence, to sort out the plants in the garden and to repair the garden gnomes. The [behaviour support] teacher recalled him saying: 'As a child I remember your wife … she used to give my sister flowers to take to mum. She was always smiling and she had a nice face.' Wiremu hugged his mother and apologized over and over again.
>
> (Wearmouth *et al.*, 2007, p. 43)

Belonging is a fundamental human need. Even the most hardened pupils will experience intense and often contradictory emotions when they are challenging school. As Furlong (1991, p. 296) comments:

> Feelings of anger, fear, frustration, elation and guilt may all be present. In the classroom the peer group may be shown the more positive side when feelings of bravado and elation may be to the fore, while in the privacy of the head teacher's office the same pupils may express guilt and remorse at their actions.

'Wiremu' might have been identified as deviant, suffering from AD/HD or labelled as something else, and charged with illegal driving of a vehicle and criminal damage to property. Instead, he kept his word, repaired the damage he had caused, and, with the support of family and community, harmony was restored. As the behaviour support teacher commented:

> There was not a dry eye in that whare [meeting-room] and I will not forget it in a hurry. The meeting ended with everyone walking away with their mana [personal standing] and wairua [sense of spiritual well-being] strengthened by what they had seen.
>
> (Wearmouth *et al.*, 2007, p. 43)

CONCLUSION

Antisocial or challenging behaviour in classrooms and around the school is sometimes explained as a problem that stems from the student him/herself and his/her family or circumstances. This may be the case with some students. However, student behaviour in schools does not occur in a vacuum. All students' behaviours are situated in a social context and result from interactions between people and their environments or social events. Participation in school activities involves the whole person in its combination of doing, talking, feeling, thinking and belonging. It refers both to taking part in activity and also to the connections with others during this process. Personal identity in schools is constituted in the way in which learners participate in activities with others and, therefore, by definition, non-participation. The implication is that the most important concern should be first to establish effective whole class management and positive classroom learning environments in which individual disruptive behaviour is much less likely to happen. Often individual students are blamed for their own failure and/or disturbing behaviour in schools rather than looking to explanations at the way society is structured to favour some children, or at the level of school structure, organisation, curriculum and classroom management. This has meant that there has been no real pressure to change society's ills or to make schools more responsive to students' needs (Armstrong, 1994, pp. 141–2).

6

UNDERSTANDING AND ADDRESSING SENSORY AND/OR PHYSICAL DIFFICULTIES AND NEEDS

INTRODUCTION

This chapter focuses on sensory and physical difficulties. Particular attention is given to hearing and/or visual impairments (VIs) and physical and motor difficulties to illustrate:

- what research studies tell us about these difficulties, including common indicators;
- the relationship between sensory and/or physical difficulties and needs and young people's learning and future life chances;
- ways that the barriers to learning experienced by young people with these difficulties can be addressed in school and elsewhere.

The frame of reference applied to assessing difficulties is generally taken from the identification and assessment of the extent of the child's sensory or physical impairment. However, as Miller and Ockleford (2005) comment, young people are individuals with different interests, background experiences and so on. As in other areas of special educational needs in schools, a whole range of information is needed to ensure that support for an individual is appropriate. This includes the views of the child and the parents/family, medical and school records.

HEARING IMPAIRMENTS

THE EAR AND HOW IT WORKS

The ear has two main functions. It receives sound and converts it into signals that the brain can understand. It also helps us to balance.

The hearing system consists of three parts, the outer, middle and inner ear, all of which must work well to allow sound to be heard properly. The outside part of the ear, known as the pinna, catches sound waves and directs them down the ear canal to the eardrum. The sound waves cause the eardrum to vibrate and the vibrations are passed across the middle ear by three tiny bones, the hammer, anvil and stirrup. These bones increase the strength of the vibrations before they pass into an organ called the cochlea in the inner ear. The cochlea is filled with fluid and contains thousands of tiny hair-like sound-sensitive cells. The vibrations entering the cochlea cause the fluid and sound-sensitive cells to move. As these cells move, they create a small electrical charge. The auditory nerve carries these signals to the brain where they are interpreted as sound. Impaired hearing occurs when one or more parts of the system is not working effectively.

BALANCE

The semicircular canals in the inner ear are three tubes, filled with liquid and movement-sensitive hair cells. As we move, the fluid moves and creates signals that are sent to the brain about balance.

DEGREES OF DEAFNESS

There are different degrees of deafness. Most often these are classified as mild, moderate, severe or profound (Spencer and Marschark, 2010). Few children are totally deaf. Most deaf children can hear some sounds at certain pitches and volume.

DIFFERENT TYPES AND CAUSES OF DEAFNESS

Deafness can be of different types. Conductive deafness is when sound cannot pass efficiently through the outer and middle ear to the cochlea and auditory nerve. The most common type of conductive deafness in children is caused by 'glue ear' (NDCS, 2010). Glue ear is a build-up of fluid in the middle ear which affects about one in five children at any time. For most children, the glue ear clears up by itself. A few need surgery to insert 'grommets' into the eardrums, tiny plastic tubes that allow air to circulate in the middle ear and help to prevent the build-up of fluid.

Sensori-neural deafness is permanent and occurs when there is a fault in the inner ear or auditory (hearing) nerve.

There are many reasons why a child can be born deaf or become deaf early in life. Around half the deaf children born in the United Kingdom every year are deaf for a genetic reason. Deafness can also be caused by complications during pregnancy. Infections, for example rubella and herpes can cause a child to be born deaf. Premature babies are often more liable to infections that can cause deafness. Severe, jaundice, a lack of oxygen at some point can also cause deafness. Infections such as meningitis, measles and mumps, a head injury or exposure to loud noises can damage the hearing system (World Health Organisation, 2010).

A major problem with late identification of deafness is the effect on language development (Goldberg and Richberg, 2004; Moeller *et al.*, 2007). A delay in identification can mean a delay in establishing effective communication with the child. This in turn can have a long-term impact on their social and educational development. The consequences on development of undetected hearing impairment may be long lasting (Yoshinaga-Itano, 2003). Children who do not hear clearly or whose hearing varies may be late to start talking, have difficulties with speech sounds, or fail to develop good listening skills. They may also have poor memory and language-processing skills, poor basic vocabularies as a result, reading and spelling problems, difficulty with sentence structure and comprehension, and achieve lower attainments in reading and mathematics. Pupils with a conductive hearing loss have a higher tendency to behaviour problems, poor motivation and attention, shyness and withdrawal (Spencer and Marschark, 2010). The most vulnerable are those whose conductive deafness started in early infancy and persisted undiagnosed for long periods.

INCLUDING CHILDREN WITH HEARING IMPAIRMENTS IN MAINSTREAM SCHOOLS

In 1908, regulations by the Board of Education in England and Wales laid down that teachers in schools for the blind and deaf must obtain within two years of their appointment an approved qualification. The 1908 regulations have broadly continued to the present day. These days many children with sensory impairments are in mainstream schools. It is essential, therefore, that teachers understand how to include them most sensitively and effectively.

Key to successful inclusion is the ethos of the school in which the hearing-impaired students are placed. The Royal National Institute for the Deaf (RNID, 2004) strongly promotes the message that effective pedagogy for students who experience hearing difficulties is effective pedagogy for a whole range of other students also. They state that 'Reviewing and adapting teaching styles, presentation methods, listening conditions and differentiation of the curriculum to address the needs of deaf pupils will also improve the learning conditions for many other pupils in the school' (ibid., p. 8).

There are three major 'types' of approach: Auditory-Oral (or 'Oral/Aural'), Sign Bilingual or Total Communication. While professionals may well be committed to one particular approach 'generally the evidence for any one method working better than another for deaf children as a whole is unclear, and all the approaches can point to some evidence which shows successful outcomes for children' (NDCS, 2010, p. 45). As the National Deaf Children's Society goes on to comment:

> The 'best' communication approach for any child and family is the one which works for them, both fitting in with the family's culture and values and most importantly, allowing the child to develop good self-esteem, a positive self-image, successful relationships, and to achieve her potential in all aspects of her life.
>
> (2010, p. 50)

Auditory-Oral approaches emphasise the use of amplification such as hearing aids, cochlear implants and radio aids to maximise the use of the child's 'residual' hearing (Spencer and Marshark, 2006). The philosophy behind auditory-oral approaches is that oral language better supports the development of reading and writing, because written language is built on an understanding of the sounds and structure of the spoken language (Beattie, 2006). The aim of this approach therefore is that deaf children should learn to use whatever residual hearing they may have to develop good listening and speaking skills which will enable them to communicate and mix with hearing people as part of the wider hearing community. The most widely used of these approaches is the Natural Aural Approach promoted by the Deaf Education through Speaking and Listening organisation. Here no sign language is used and children are not encouraged to rely on lip-reading (Lewis, 1996).

Sign Bilingualism uses sign language as the child's first language and the spoken language of the family is learned as a second language (Moores, 2008). In Sign Bilingualism in the United Kingdom, the languages are British Sign Language (BSL) (or Irish Sign Language in Ireland) and whatever is the spoken language of the home. A sign bilingual approach to developing communication is rooted in the belief that a visual language is essential for deaf children to have full access to language learning, education, information and the world around them, together with a strong positive deaf identity.

BSL is a complete language in its own right with its own grammar and linguistic rules. There is no written form. Its grammar is very different from English, so it is not used simultaneously with spoken language. BSL has developed over hundreds of years as a visual language which uses body language, head position, facial expressions and gesture as well as the hands. It also uses fingerspelling for some words which have no signs, such as names. BSL is the language of the UK Deaf community and it is estimated that about 70,000 people use it as their first or preferred language. Use of BSL can therefore bring with it a connection with Deaf culture and the opportunity and expectation of taking part in the Deaf community as well as the hearing world (Burman *et al.*, 2006). When a child uses BSL, it is useful if the rest of the family, as well as classmates and teachers in school, learn to sign.

Total communication is based on the principle that deaf children can learn to communicate effectively by using any and all means that they can in whatever combination works best: sign, speech and hearing, fingerspelling, gesture, facial expression, lip-reading and cued speech. Signed/Signs Supported English is a sign support system which uses signs taken from BSL, together with fingerspelling (Moores, 2001). It is used in the word order of English to supplement what is being spoken. Signed English, similarly, uses signs taken from BSL together with some specially developed 'markers' made with the hands, and fingerspelling, to give an exact representation of the word order and the grammar of English through sign. It is mainly used to support the teaching of reading and writing. In fingerspelling, each letter of the alphabet is indicated by using the fingers and palm of the hand (Padden and Gunsals, 2003). It is used to support Sign Language to spell names and places and for words that do not have an established BSL sign. Lip-reading is the process of reading words from the lip patterns of the person speaking (Spencer and Marschark, 2010). For a number of reasons, lip-reading is never enough on its own. Many speech sounds are not visible on the lips. Lip patterns also vary from person to person. Further, lack of clarity around the face, for example poor lighting conditions, beards or moustaches that obscure the mouth, or eating while talking can make lip-reading difficult. Lip-reading therefore is used to support other communication approaches. Cued Speech is a sound-based system that accompanies natural speech and uses eight hand shapes in four different positions (cues) to represent the sounds of English visually (Hage and Leybaert, 2006). Some spoken sounds cannot be fully lip-read: 'p', 'm' and 'b' all look the same on the lips; sounds like 'd', 'k' and 'g' cannot be seen on the lips. Hand shapes are 'cued' near to the mouth to make clear the sounds of English which look the same when lip-read. It is intended to make every sound and word clear to deaf children and therefore enable them to have full access to spoken language. The association between the sounds and letters of spoken English is intended to help develop literacy skills as well as spoken language.

ASSISTIVE DEVICES

As the NDCS (2008, p. 31) comments, deaf children often use assistive listening devices to assist them to hear what a speaker is saying, particularly in noisy listening conditions. Personal FM systems (often known as radio aids) are very useful, especially at school, college or at home. 'They can help reduce effects of background noise in, for example, a school classroom, and help a child to concentrate on one person's voice, often their teacher.' Radio aids have a transmitter with a microphone and a receiver. The person talking wears the transmitter and the sounds are transmitted by radio waves to the receiver. The deaf child wears the receiver which picks up the signal from the transmitter and converts it back to sound. The child's hearing aids or implants amplify the sound so that the child can hear what is said.

Classroom sound field systems are designed for similar reasons as radio aids, but are not the same. A sound field system includes a microphone worn by the speaker that is linked to an amplifier by either an FM radio transmitter or an infrared transmitter so that the speaker can walk around a room with no need for wires. Loudspeakers are fitted around the room. The sound field system amplifies the speaker's voice to produce a clear, consistent level of sound above the background noise (NDCS, 2008). Most children with hearing aids or cochlear implants will still need to use a radio aid in a classroom with a sound field system.

Sound waves reverberate and increase the amount of background noise in rooms with hard surfaces (Moeller *et al.*, 2007). Sound field systems and the acoustic treatment of teaching spaces can improve the listening environment for all students. It is important for class teachers to think carefully about the clarity of their spoken language (Wilkins and Ertmer, 2002). Teachers should use natural speech patterns and not exaggerate lip movements or shout, highlight key terms and key concepts and place themselves in a position appropriate for students to lip-read or benefit from a hearing aid where the maximum range is often 2 m. Deaf students may also need to be encouraged to see the faces of peers who are speaking. To acquire spoken and written English, students may also need the support of visual and written forms of language, as well as lip-reading or multisensory clues (Harris and Moreno, 2006). For example, with video materials, deaf students might benefit with advanced access to a summary of the programme and new vocabulary and concepts explained, as well as subtitles. In addition, auditory-oral approaches require 'consistent, efficient use of individual hearing aids, radio aids and/or cochlear implant devices' (RNID, 2004, p. 15).

As the RNID (2004, p. 15) notes, in 2000 the vast majority of all deaf children in English schools were reported to be using 'auditory-oral' approaches that do 'not use sign language or manually coded elements to support the understanding of spoken language'. These approaches assume that students have enough residual hearing to acquire and use spoken language without needing to use sign language or fingerspelling, provided there is sufficient amplification of sound. Although some children make progress that is commensurate with their age, as Spencer and Marshark (2006) comment, many do not keep pace with hearing peers.

The listening environment is a crucial consideration (Spencer and Marschark, 2010). Intensity or loudness is measured in decibels (dB). Frequency (pitch) is measured in Hertz (Hz). All sounds are made up of different frequencies. Speech comprises vowels and consonants. Vowel sounds are low frequency and consonants are generally higher in frequency. Speech is usually a mix of high- and low-frequency sounds. The main issue for schools is that everyday building materials absorb the higher frequency sounds more easily than lower frequency sounds. This means that the consonants, which are required for speech clarity, are more likely to be absorbed than the vowels. Therefore additional special materials may need to be added to a room to absorb more of the lower frequency sounds (Moeller *et al.*, 2007). Noise in classrooms is mostly speech, mainly low frequency. If enough is reflected it masks important high-frequency consonants making it difficult to understand what the teacher is saying. As much low-frequency reflection as possible therefore needs to be prevented.

COMMUNICATING WITH DEAF CHILDREN

The National Deaf Children's Society (NDCS) (2010, pp. 10–2) offers useful advice to teachers and families of children with hearing impairments. For example it advises avoiding competing noise in the background that makes hearing difficult, bringing everyday sounds to the child's conscious attention and helping the child make the connection between the object and the sound it is making by looking at it. In the home it might be a vacuum cleaner. At school it might be the bell. Carpets, curtains and soft furnishings that do not reflect sound, are more 'acoustically friendly' than wooden or ceramic flooring and blinds. The RNID also suggests staying within the child's vision, as much as possible to enable the child to use visual clues from body language, including facial expressions and lip-reading, and not placing the child facing the window so that s/he is looking into bright light. Wearing plain rather than patterned clothes means that the child can see the signed communication more easily. Visual supports, such as objects, books, toys, or pictures, can help children to understand unfamiliar concepts. Deaf children's attention should be drawn to the variety of interactions and forms of communication going on around them. If everyone around deaf children uses signing with each other as well as with the children they can interpret verbal interactions between everyone around. People speaking to deaf children should face them repeat and rephrase if they do not understand. Most importantly, adults and peers should respond to their attempts to communicate and, not speak for them.

VISUAL IMPAIRMENT

As discussed in Chapter 7 on assessment, VI is a general term that indicates a continuum of sight loss (Mason *et al.*, 1997). VI is estimated to affect around 25,000 children in the United Kingdom (Tate *et al.*, 2005). At least 4 in every 10,000 children born in the United Kingdom are diagnosed as severely visually impaired or blind by their first birthday (Miller and Ockleford, 2005). VI might be the result of the following: genetic or hereditary illness, including congenital optic nerve and retinal disorders, damage to the eye before, during or sometime after birth, or damage to the visual cortex or to other areas of the brain concerned with information processing. Fifty per cent of blind and partially sighted children also have additional disabilities and this includes 30 per cent with severe or profound and multiple learning difficulties.

Around 3 per cent of blind and partially sighted pupils, aged 5–16, used Braille as their sole or main format for reading and writing (Morris and Smith, 2008).

INCLUDING PUPILS WITH A VISUAL IMPAIRMENT IN THE CLASSROOM

As a result of their visual difficulties, before going to school children may well have had less opportunity to explore their environment and learn through observing and copying the actions of others (Douglas and McLinden, 2005). Both academic progress and children's social skills may be influenced by this. Children may therefore need teaching of literacy development through specialist codes such as Braille or Moon or through print/modified print Braille, and/or specialist teaching of mobility, tactile and keyboard skills, as well as social and life skills generally. It is important to consider whether and when to withdraw the child from the mainstream classroom for specialist or additional teaching so that the pupil does not become socially isolated and the mainstream teacher maintains full responsibility for the pupil.

Davis (2003) notes that visually impaired children may become very tired as a result of the amount of concentration required to complete tasks, and/or need more time to complete tasks. Special consideration of the learning environment, in particular the classroom, may well be necessary, for example where to site quiet or loud areas, Braille and/or tactile/large print signs, bulky equipment such as CCTV, a Brailler and computers, as well as classroom lighting (Mason, 2001).

Braille is the alphabet and numbers, designed to be read by fingers rather than eyes through a series of raised dots on a page. The RNIB (2010) notes that a blind French schoolboy, Louis Braille, devised the code more than 200 years ago. This code is based on six dots arranged in two columns of three. Different types of Braille codes use combinations of these dots, 63 in all, to represent letters of the alphabet, numbers, punctuation marks and common letter groups (Figure 6.1).

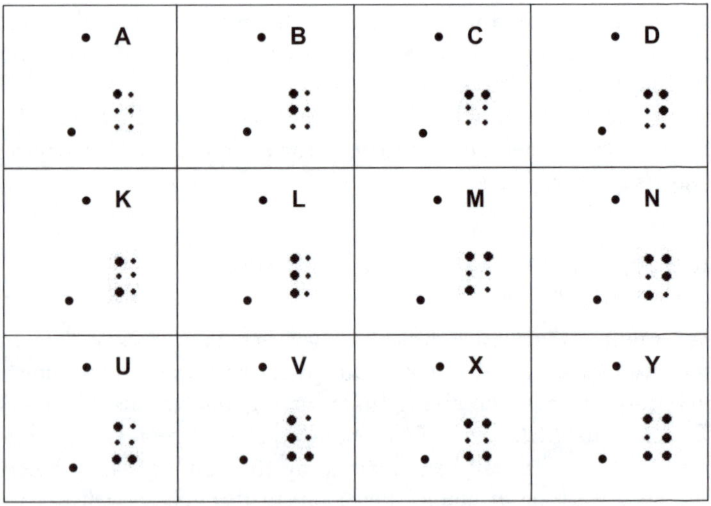

Figure 6.1 Braille alphabet

There are two grades of Braille: uncontracted (previously Grade 1) and contracted (previously Grade 2). Uncontracted includes a letter for letter and number for number translation from print. Contracted has special signs for common words and letter combinations. This usually increases the speed of reading. Particular subject areas, for example music, mathematics, science and foreign languages, have their own specialist codes.

The RNIB (op cit) gives examples of reading schemes where printed books

> have been adapted to include either uncontracted Braille (grade 1) or contracted Braille (grade 2) on interleaved clear plastic sheets, so that the pictures and print story can be seen underneath. This enables shared reading between sighted and blind readers.

as it is clearly useful for parent and child, teacher and child, and/or friends to share books.

There are a number of common misconceptions about VI, for example, as Mason (2001, p. 20) points out, holding a book close will not harm vision. Dim light will not harm eyes. Some conditions, for example albinism, mean that a child may require a low level of lighting. Having a VI does not mean that other senses, for example hearing or touch, are highly developed.

As Mason also comments, in order to plan appropriate support for pupils with VI, teachers and support staff need to consider whether the child has a preferred or dominant eye or a defect in field or colour vision. This is important for both seating and using appropriate teaching strategies. There may well be restrictions on physical activities which may constrain the child's participation with peers. Low vision aids may have been prescribed, so it is important to know when they should be used and whether the child has been trained to use them. Also, a consideration of lighting levels as well as size and contrast of print is important to maximise the child's vision.

MULTI-SENSORY IMPAIRMENT

Multi-sensory impairment means difficulty with both vision and hearing. Children with multi-sensory impairment may be born with it or acquire it later as a result of illness or injury. Very few children are totally blind and deaf. In the past Rubella (German measles) during pregnancy was a main cause of deaf-blindness. However, as a result of vaccination against Rubella usually before girls reach the age of puberty it is now uncommon. Premature birth and/or severe infections during early childhood may also cause deaf-blindness.

The reduced and possibly distorted visual and auditory information that pupils with multi-sensory impairment receive means that they have limited and possibly confused experience of the world (Aitken, 2000). Some children become skilled at using touch as a means of learning about the world and a means of communicating. Others may become skilled in using the sense of smell. Others may sense movement around them from differences in air pressure. Taylor (2007, p. 205) notes the difficulties experiences by many of these children in communicating:

> These include: a reduced and confused experience of the world, becoming passive and isolated, and the tendency to be echolalic or repeating the last word said to them, all of which limit their ability to make choices. Aitken and Millar (2002) also highlight the effects of hearing impairment on individuals' communication, including isolation from information and from other people. A physical impairment in association with communication difficulties will also present additional challenges. The child with MSI has all these difficulties compounded.

BILL

Bill, aged 14, had quadriplegic cerebral palsy, which caused weakness in all limbs, and epilepsy. His left arm and hand had some useful function for picking up objects, signing and gesturing. He had bilateral optic atrophy and was registered blind, with some peripheral vision in his left eye. He also had a conductive hearing loss. Other people communicated with him mainly through speech, objects and signing on the body, and expressively through sign, gesture, and vocalisation. He used a voice output communication aid (VOCA) to relay messages from home to school and to make some choices.

(Taylor, 2007, p. 206)

For those young people whose visual and vocal ability is severely affected, many assistive devices are available to enable students to communicate: electronic language boards, voice synthesisers and voice recognition software.

MULTI-SENSORY TEACHING

Multi-sensory teaching is simultaneous use of visual, auditory and kinesthetic-tactile senses to enhance memory and learning. Links are consistently made between the visual (what we see), auditory (what we hear) and kinesthetic-tactile (movement and feeling) pathways in learning to read and spell.

The use of such an approach for children whose senses are compromised or greatly reduced could be effective if careful planning takes account of their individual sensory strengths. Using a multi-sensory teaching approach means helping a child to learn through more than one of the senses. One possible approach is to involve the use of senses that are intact, especially the use of touch and movement. This will provide the brain with tactile and kinesthetic memories to reinforce learning, as well as residual visual and auditory ones. Helen Keller is, perhaps, the best known deaf-blind child in history. A childhood had left her both blind and deaf. During the following few years, Helen became a very difficult child, with her violent outbursts, screaming and temper tantrums, born of frustration. When she was six her family found a teacher who herself was partially sighted and had been educated in an institution for visually impaired children. When she arrived, she immediately started teaching Helen to finger spell. At first Helen could not understand what Anne was trying to communicate to her. The breakthrough came when Anne pumped water over one of Helen's hands and spelled out the word 'water' in the other. Something about this made the connection between the word and its meaning. Helen made rapid progress after that. Anne taught her to read, first with raised letters and later with Braille, and to write with both ordinary and Braille typewriters.

MUSCULAR DYSTROPHY

An estimated 8,000 to 10,000 people in the United Kingdom have a form of muscular dystrophy (Pohlschmidt and Meadowcroft, 2010).

The term is used to refer to a group of genetic muscle diseases associated with progressive weakness and wasting of muscles owing to the degeneration of muscle cells. This can include the heart.

There are over 30 different conditions that can be categorised into seven groups, including Duchenne, Becker, limb girdle, congenital, facioscapulohumeral, oculopharyngeal and Emery-Dreifuss. The severity of muscular dystrophy is very variable. Symptoms can be obvious at birth or shortly thereafter. Sometimes the symptoms are very mild and are seen much later, between the ages of 40–50. Most of these involve a defect in a protein that plays a vital role in muscle cell function or repair.

To take one example, Duchenne muscular dystrophy affects only boys, with very rare exceptions. Around one boy in 35,000 is born with this condition – that is, about 100 boys born in the United Kingdom each year. In just over 50 per cent of all cases the mother carries the gene but is usually not herself affected by it. Each son of a carrier has a 50 per cent chance of being affected and each daughter has a 50 per cent chance of being a carrier. A problem in the genes results in a defect in dystrophin, which is an important protein in muscle fibres. Most boys with this condition develop the first signs of difficulty in walking at the age of 1–3 years and are usually unable to run or jump like their peers. By about 8–11 years boys become unable to walk. By their late teens or early twenties the muscle-wasting is severe enough to shorten life expectancy (Pohlschmidt and Meadowcroft, 2010).

Regular supervision from a clinic is very important to manage the condition as effectively as possible. Many children who experience difficulties in gross motor movement may use a wheelchair. Others may be unable to control or vary their posture efficiently.

> These children will need specialised equipment to aid their mobility, to support their posture and to protect and restore their body shape, muscle tone and quality of life. It is vital that children with physical needs have access to appropriate forms of therapy, for example physiotherapy and hydrotherapy, and that their carers receive training to enable them to manage their physical needs confidently on a day-to-day basis.
>
> (Mencap, undated, p. 5)

The kinds of physical access supported by ICT can considerably reduce physical barriers to the learning of some students. For example, a student who cannot use his/her hands can control the computer by pressing a switch with his/her head.

> A youngster who has problems with fine motor control can use a track-erball to move a pointer across the screen. He can select the options in a drawing package to draw a series of geometric shapes, with a confidence that the quality of the results will do justice to his intentions.
>
> (NCET, 1995, p. 4)

THE EXAMPLE OF MICHAEL

Michael was a young 9-year-old boy with Duchenne muscular dystrophy who featured in an Open University video programme (Open University, 2000). He was a pupil in a mainstream primary school and participated in lessons in the same way as peers. A full-time learning support assistant was appointed to take care of his personal hygiene needs in school and to help him move around generally. For example, at his request she held up his hand in the classroom when he wanted to answer a question. There was a very close collaborative working relationship between her and Michael's family. Various members of outside agencies were involved in his health, well-being and academic progress. For example, he was monitored very carefully by a physiotherapist for signs of increasing problems with his mobility, and had regular physiotherapy in school time to alleviate as far as possible the development of contractures, that is the shortening of his muscles. A member of the local authority learning support team visited the school regularly to check whether he had appropriate equipment to meet his needs, for example a laptop with peripherals that enabled him to connect to the computer easily as well as appropriate software to access the primary curriculum.

RESONDING TO THE NEEDS OF PUPILS WITH SEVERE DIFFICULTIES IN MOTOR MOVEMENT

Individual children with severe motor difficulties:

> may have difficulties affecting some or all of their limbs, limited hand function, fine and gross motor difficulties and sometimes difficulties with speech and language. Most, though not all pupils will have a

medical diagnosis. A diagnosis may have been given at birth, at about the age of two or a later date, though deteriorating conditions such as muscular dystrophy may not be diagnosed until the child attends school. Some children may have physical difficulties as a result of an accident or illness, which can happen at any age. It must be remembered that, in the same way as other children, they may also have learning difficulties, dyslexia, dyspraxia, asthma, epilepsy, vision and hearing difficulties or hidden handicaps affecting their visual/auditory perception or eye/hand co-ordination etc.

(Pickles, 2001, p. 290)

A long-term plan for these pupils would take into account

dignity and emotional needs ... especially in positioning, toileting and transfers ... to enable pupils to be as independent as possible ... recognising that teaching methods may need to vary as needs change is all part of inclusion.

(Ibid., p. 292)

It would also need to include views of the student as a person, with hopes, expectations and rights, considerations of physical access to the school environment, ways in which the needs of the family and the student's place within it can be taken into account by the school, the role of the support assistant(s) and the kind of relationship that might be established with the student and the family, and any issues this raises and the role and function of information and communications technology and of any other appropriate technological aids. How therapy might fit into the child's curriculum might also be very important. Staff in the school, and peers if appropriate, would need to be made aware of the child's strengths and needs.

LIAISING WITH SUPPORT STAFF

In general terms, one of the ways of approaching how to support students who experience visual, auditory or physical difficulties is to consider how best to liaise with support staff who may be employed to help address these students' learning needs. The Education (Specified Work and Registration) (England) Regulations 2003 specify circumstances in which certain kinds of school staff – such as support staff – may carry out 'specified work' relating to teaching and learning. 'Specified work' includes planning, preparing and delivering lessons to students, assessing and reporting on the development, individuals as well as groups. The role of support staff in the classroom is to help the teacher make sure that each student engages positively in class activities and makes progress. Support staff can help to support the development of differentiated curricular approaches to meet the diversity of students' learning needs.

SUMMARY

The greatest challenge for a child with a sensory impairment is communication (Spencer and Marschark, 2010). A child who can see and hear will reach out and explore its surroundings naturally. A child with a sensory impairment will not necessarily do this and may need encouragement to explore and interact with others. For a deaf child, normal progress in language may be hard. Intensive education and support may be needed throughout the child's life. Early intervention in the child's life is clearly very important. A unique communication method may be developed for the child but whatever the means of communication it should enable that child to develop cognitive and other skills, whether it is symbols, objects of reference, sign language, Braille or something else.

However much is known about a child's sensory of physical difficulties though, as Miller and Ockleford (2005) aptly comment, that child is still an individual with his/her own personal strengths and needs, interests, experiences, background, and so on that, together with his/her own views, must all be taken into account when drawing up any intervention plan.

7

ASSESSMENT AND PLANNING FOR CHILDREN WITH SPECIAL EDUCATIONAL NEEDS

INTRODUCTION

This chapter will open by explaining how some children can be supported to make huge learning gains and, consequently, will feel much more positively about themselves as learners if teachers, parents and others clearly understand the power of some forms of assessment, monitoring and focussed feedback. It will continue by discussing the following topics:

- principles of different kinds of assessment of difficulties in learning
  - o summative and standardised,
  - o ongoing formative assessment and constructive feedback to students,
  - o criterion referenced assessment;
- ways of assessing behaviour experienced as problematic or challenging, including assessments from a biological and/or medical perspective;
- assessment of sensory impairments;
- the significance of understanding the barriers to learning from the student's and family's perspective;
- framework for planning;
- developing, implementing, monitoring and evaluating an individual education plan (IEP) examples of IEPs to address different experiences of difficulties at different ages and stages.

THE PLACE OF ASSESSMENT IN SUPPORTING LEARNING AND BEHAVIOUR NEEDS

In education generally, and certainly in the area of special educational needs, there are a number of different frames of reference for conceptualising how a child's learning and behaviour and the difficulties that are experienced should be assessed and, therefore, what the starting point might be for developing appropriate ways to meet that child's learning or behavioural needs. For example, deciding whether a child's need is 'special' by definition means using a form of assessment, often very formal, summative by nature and standardised against national norms, that enables comparison with the learning achievement and behaviour patterns of peers, or norms for sight, hearing, movement and so on. After all, by law, a child has a learning difficulty if 'he [sic] has a significantly greater difficulty in learning than the majority of children of his age' (Education Act 1996, S. 312) and the educational provision that is required to meet the needs is 'special'. There are some obvious questions raised by this definition, for example how to measure 'significantly greater difficulty in learning', how to compare one student to the majority, how to gauge the contexts in which what is already provided is insufficient so that appropriate provision is therefore 'special' and how to ensure that a child whose attainment levels are demonstrated to be very poor in comparison with peers does not feel so demoralised that she/he will not try any more. There is plenty of evidence to indicate that assessment itself can serve to reinforce or undermine the motivation to strive for future achievement in schools (Murphy, 2002).

We do not always wish to compare one child with others, however. It is always important to have a sense of children's ongoing progress in learning through ongoing continuous formative assessment that can provide teachers and others with opportunities to notice what is happening during learning activities, recognise the level and direction of the learning of individuals and see how they can help to take that learning further.

Sometimes also we need to know whether a child has reached a particular threshold or level in his/her learning. So-called criterion referencing means comparing a child's achievements with clearly stated criteria for learning outcomes and clear descriptors of particular levels of performance within them. Setting out criteria for an assessment clarifies not only both what is required of learners but also assists teachers or others in deciding what they need to teach. Criterion referencing can also improve the quality of feedback offered to learners as the descriptors of levels of performance and the overall criteria should be clear enough to serve as indicators of what learners have to do to succeed (Wearmouth, 2009).

Anyone considering assessing a child needs to be fully conversant with test procedures, their aims and rationale as well as wider cultural and social factors, the school, the area of the curriculum concerned and also attributes of the individual child and above all, of course, what useful information the assessment can give.

FORMAL, NORM-REFERENCED (STANDARDISED) TESTS

Identification of the students who are 'different' and, therefore, who is eligible for special educational provision may depend on the results of norm-referenced assessment that is designed to indicate a learner's achievement in comparison with others. Whatever is assessed here has to be measurable, otherwise it is not possible to compare one child's score with another. For example, it is very common to use norm-referenced tests in the area of reading. One example is the Neale Analysis of Reading Ability (Neale, 1997) which provides normative scores in both reading accuracy and comprehension.

To understand the use and, potentially, misuse, of standardised testing it is important to understand the test standardisation process, as well as a number of important concepts related to standardised tests and test procedures: 'measure of spread' of scores, validity and reliability, the usefulness of standardised scores and interpretations of percentile ranks, confidence bands and reading ages.

THE STANDARDISATION PROCESS

One way to make test scores such as 21 out of 36 more readily understandable and comparable another test score such as 11 out of 30 would be to convert them to percentages (58 and 37 per cent, to the nearest whole number). However, these percentages on their own do not tell us either the average score of all children taking the same tests and therefore how well or badly children are doing in comparison with peers, or how spread out the scores are. Standardising a test score involves assessing a large, nationally representative sample using that particular test and then adjusting the mean (average) to a score of 100. It is easy to compare a child's result with this score of 100.

An important concept associated with standardised tests is that of the 'measure of the spread' of scores, the so-called standard deviation. This is usually set to 15 for educational attainment and ability tests. Irrespective of the difficulty of the test, about 68 per cent of students in a national sample will have a standardised score within one standard deviation (15 points) of the average (i.e. between 85–115) and about 95 per cent will have a standardised score within two standard deviations (30 points) of the average (between 70–130). These examples come from a frequency distribution, known as the 'normal distribution', which is shown in Figure 7.1.

VALIDITY AND RELIABILITY

The terms 'validity' and 'reliability' are often used in relation to both formal and informal tests. In general, the 'validity' of a test is the degree to which that test assesses what it is intended to test. We might ask, for example whether a test of cognitive ability or reading that has been developed and standardised in Britain would be valid for young people from a completely different culture and new to the United Kingdom, or how valid is the concept of 'reading age' and whether and/or how this might relate to adults. We might also ask whether the test tests what we expect it to test in the context in which it is being used, in other words whether a test has 'context validity'.

'Reliability', on the other hand, generally means whether we would obtain the same result on the same test with the same cohort of individuals if we did the test procedure again.

USEFULNESS OF STANDARDISED SCORES

The use of standardised scores is often thought to be useful for a number of reasons. First, it produces a scale that enables a comparison of results so that we can see whether a child is above or below the national average. The date when the test was standardised is important here, however. An old test might well be out of date in

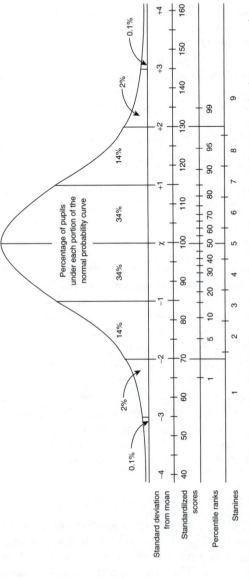

Figure 7.1 The relationship between standardised scores, percentile ranks and stanines under a normal distribution curve

terms of comparisons of individuals with national norms. Re-standardisation of an old test might well give different national norms in relation to the current generation of children. Second, scores are standardised so that the ages of the children are taken into account. When looking at a child's score on a standardised assessment against national norms, we will be able to tell whether that child is above or below other children of the same age. Third, using standardised scores allows us to compare a child's performance on a test in one area of the curriculum, for example reading, with another, for example mathematics. Or we might compare a child's performance in two different aspects of the same area, for example reading comprehension and reading accuracy, which might be important in assessing whether a child is dyslexic.

PERCENTILE RANKS

There is a constant relationship between percentile ranks and standardised scores when the same average score and standard deviation are used. The percentile rank is the percentage of students in the sample of the same age who gained a score *at the same level or below* that of the child's score. So performance at the 50th percentile indicates that the child performed as well as, or better than 50 per cent of the sample when age is taken into account.

CONFIDENCE BANDS

'Confidence bands' indicate the range of scores within which the accurate assessment of attainment is likely to fall. It is not possible to obtain the 'true score', that is the hypothetically perfect measurement of the individual's ability. Tests of the sort discussed here measure attainment, that is, the outcome of the student's work at any particular time, not 'ability'. In addition, however carefully educational tests are put together and administered, errors can result from factors such as the child's state of health, tiredness, lack of familiarity with formal assessments and so on.

THE CONCEPT OF 'READING AGE'

The concept of 'reading age' is a very commonly used concept in relation to norm-referenced assessments of literacy learning, for example in standardised assessments such as the Neale Analysis of Reading Ability (Neale, 1997). Reading age indicates the age at which a given raw score was the average. It is obtained by working out for each age group the average raw score of all of the children in the sample of that age and then smoothing out any irregularities in the resulting graph. Increases in performance with age are smaller for older age groups. This raises issues for using this measurement with older students, because accuracy and rate of reading would show no improvement beyond a certain point.

Reading ages represent snapshots of a progression in literacy development. They are not fixed and exact measures of reading attainment. Reading is a learned behaviour that is closely aligned with development and age. Thus a low reading score does not necessarily suggest general low ability, slow developmental growth and so on. However, if we use these normative scores while taking into account the confidence bands attributed to the known score we can then view reading ages as estimates of reading ability at the time of testing.

ISSUES ASSOCIATED WITH NORM-REFERENCING

Standardised tests alone are not designed to diagnose the root of difficulties in learning experienced by a learner. Anyone considering assessing a child needs to be fully conversant with test procedures, their aims and rationale as well as wider cultural and social factors, the school, the area of the curriculum concerned and also attributes of the individual child and above all, of course, what useful information the assessment can give. Additionally there are a number of issues associated with normative assessment including equity and the link between achievement norms and teacher expectations of particular learners.

First, in relation to the question of equity, some students may be allocated additional resources after achieving only very low scores on norm-referenced tests. However, there is a very grey area around the cut-off point above which other students will receive no additional provision.

Then there is the issue that when an individual student's test score lies within the bottom 'tail' of a normal distribution curve there is often an assumption that the student's innate ability is very low. Using standardised forms of tests means that we can pinpoint those students whose scores fall into the lowest 2 per cent or so. However, poor scores on normative tests can also mean that students' failure to achieve in school is automatically 'blamed' on poor ability, or the family, or the ethnic group. Sometimes this is known as the 'deficit' view of children who experience difficulties. This view can limit teachers' expectations of what to expect of certain students and, therefore, lead to continued poor achievement (Rosenthal and Jacobson, 1968). It also absolves schools from responsibility for that learner's progress in school rather than opening up discussion of how classroom teaching practices and the school curriculum generally can be adapted to suit students' learning and behaviour better. 'Success' and 'failure' on norm-referenced tests are not just the result of children's natural ability, however (Tomlinson, 1988). Some families cannot support their own children adequately as a result of the circumstances in which they find themselves and the way that schools are structured, as much as of a lack of innate ability in the child.

FORMATIVE ASSESSMENT

'There is no evidence that increasing the amount of testing will enhance learning' on its own (Assessment Reform Group, 1999, p. 2). Results from externally imposed summative tests, especially where there are very high stakes attached to these results in countries such as England, can have very negative effects on students.

Assessment can be a powerful educational tool for promoting learning but it depends on the kind of assessment that is used, and the manner of its use. In a seminal piece of work, Black and Wiliam (1998) demonstrated clearly that student achievement, particularly that of lower achievers, can be raised through formative, rather than summative, assessment in the classroom. They found that improving learning through assessment depends on five, 'deceptively simple', factors: providing effective feedback, actively involving students in their own learning, modifying teaching in response to the results of assessment, recognising the influence of assessment on students' motivation and self-esteem and enabling students to assess themselves and understand that they need to do to improve (Assessment Reform Group, 1999, p. 5). The frame of reference for this research includes the view that learners have active agency in learning. They do it for themselves. Assessment that supports learning must therefore involve students so that they have information about how well they are doing to guide subsequent learning in a constructive way that shows them what they need to do, and can do, to make progress.

The shift in emphasis in the purpose of day-to-day assessment in classrooms has resulted in a focus in many places on 'Assessment for Learning' (AfL), that is ongoing day-to-day formative assessment to collect information on what children do or do not understand and the adaptation of teaching in response to this. Ongoing day-to-day assessments include questioning and discussions with children, observations of children while they are working; holding, analysing children's work and giving quick feedback (http://nationalstrategies.standards.dcsf.gov.uk/node/88910 accessed 14 February 2011). Feedback that connects directly to specific and challenging goals related to students' prior knowledge and experience helps those students to focus more productively on new goals and next learning steps (Ministry of Education, 2005, p. 16).

CRITERION REFERENCING

Criterion referencing adopts a different frame of reference from norm-referencing. Whereas norm-referenced assessment ranks a learner against all other learners, criterion referencing compares a learner's performance against identified standards of achievement. The quality of achievement is evaluated by how well the individual learner has performed in relation to specific criteria and standards that illustrate key features of learning, achievement and quality at different stages of children's development (Dunn *et al.*, 2002). In order to enable teachers to engage in conversations that link back to and promote students' learning outcomes, some schools use authentic examples of students' work that illustrate what these criteria look like. These examples can be used by students and teachers to identify next learning steps. Teachers can compare a student's work sample with the exemplars in order to identify specific strengths and weaknesses, identify individual teaching and learning needs and prioritise new learning goals. By discussing and exemplifying a child's achievement and progress in relation to selected samples of work, parents

and caregivers can be better informed about what work at a particular curriculum level looks like and how they too can better support
the next learning steps.

ASSESSMENT OF BEHAVIOUR

Students' behaviour in schools does not occur in a vacuum (Watkins
and Wagner, 1995). Students are members of classrooms which function as aspects of the school system within particular neighbourhoods.
Students also fulfil roles within their own families and communities.
Difficult behaviour which seems to relate to a particular student may
be indicative of a range of contextual issues associated with society,
the family, ethnic or community group, school, classroom, peer group
or teacher, as well as the individual student (Wearmouth *et al.*, 2005).

Interventions designed to improve student behaviour can be
centred on the child, on the environment, on the child and the environment or on the interface between the child and their environment.
There are a number of ways of conceptualising the interactional relationship between the learning environment and the learner. For
example, from an ecosystemic perspective Bronfenbrenner (1979)
identifies four levels that influence student outcomes: *microsystem*,
the immediate context of the student – school, classrooms, home,
neighbourhood, *mesosystem*, the links between two microsystems,
for example home–school relationships, *exosystem*, outside demands
and influences in adults' lives that affect students and *macrosystem*,
cultural beliefs and patterns or government or institutional policies
that affect individuals' behaviour, including societal structure and
organisation and prevailing value systems.

Ysseldyke and Christenson (1987, 1993) argue that it is important
to assess characteristics of the classroom learning environments in
which students are placed because these can be changed to support
more effective learning. They identify a number of instructional factors in the classroom environment that influence student outcomes.
Ysseldyke and Christenson (1987, 1993) argue that it is important
also to focus assessment on current features of classroom practice
because these can be changed to support more effective learning.
They used their analysis of these features in the learning environment to design 'The Instructional Environment Scale' as a framework

for the systematic collection of data to analyse contextual barriers to students' learning. Data are gathered through classroom observation and interview with both student and teacher on 12 components of teaching: instructional presentation, classroom environment, teacher expectations, cognitive emphasis, motivational strategies, relevant practice, academic engaged time, informed feedback, adaptive instruction, progress evaluation, instructional planning and student understanding (Ysseldyke and Christenson, 1987, p. 21).

COLLECTING EVIDENCE OF INDIVIDUAL CHILDREN'S BEHAVIOUR

Observing children in the environment of the classroom or school is something that is a part of teachers' everyday practice. It is rare, however, for teachers to have the opportunity to stand back and closely observe the processes, relationships and behaviours involved in teaching and learning. For the purposes of assessment of individual students' behaviour, this process might need to be formalised. If so, it should be systematic and there should be an effective means of recording and interpreting what is seen.

One way to approach this issue is to adopt a problem-solving frame of reference to identify when the challenges presented by an individual student's behaviour require special consideration. In order to develop effective problem solving, Watkins and Wagner (1995, p. 59) pose a number of questions: What specific behaviour is causing concern? In what situations does the behaviour occur/not occur? What, specifically, happens before and after the behaviour (i.e. what triggers it and what maintains it?) What skills does the person demonstrate/not demonstrate? What does the person's behaviour mean to him/her? What does the person think of him/herself and what do others think? Who is most affected by this behaviour? The last question often turns attention from the behaviour causing concern to the way the concern is being handled by others.

OBSERVATION OF BEHAVIOUR

Bell (1999) points out that, while direct observation of young people's behaviour is not an easy option – it requires careful organisation and practice – nonetheless it can reveal characteristics of the behaviour of groups or individuals which would have been impossible to discover by other means. Direct observation can be particularly useful to find out whether people do what they say, behave in the way they claim to behave, or that other people claim they behave.

As Fisher *et al.* (2004) comment, there are a number of different formats that can be adopted. The first step is to make decisions about exactly *what* will be the focus of the observation: people, activities or events or a combination of these. It might be important to observe an individual, a group or a whole class in particular lessons or playground activities. If the problem-solving approach recommended by Watkins and Wagner (1995) is adopted, observations may take place in specific, preselected lessons or locations where individual students' behaviour has been identified as particularly problematic. Then, as Fisher *et al.* (2004) go on to note, there is a question about the time frames to be used: whether to sample what goes on during short predetermined time periods or whether an individual student will be 'shadowed' for a longer period of time. The answers to these questions will, to a large extent, be dictated by the kinds of concerns raised in relation to the behaviour of individual students, the kinds of reflection that has already taken place in relation to the evidence already collected and the extent to which an audit of the learning environment such as that framed by Ysseldyke and Christenson (1987, 1993) has already formed part of the collection of evidence.

When conducting observations, it is usually more helpful to make notes at the time, even if systematic time sampling or event recording procedures are being implemented. These notes might be open ended, where general points of interest are recorded or can be focussed on targeted events as and when they happen. A useful format is to write down what happened, and then to add a brief comment or interpretation later. If the observer is looking for particular events or behaviours which can be easily categorised, she/he could devise an 'observation schedule'. Systematic observation procedures might involve the construction of a grid in which instances of specified learner, peer and adult behaviours can be recorded as they occur.

FUNCTIONAL ASSESSMENT OF INDIVIDUAL BEHAVIOUR

One of the questions posed by Watkins and Wagner above relates to the gain for the individual (i.e. the function that is served) by behaving in a particular way. Functional analysis can be seen as an experimental approach to behavioural assessment in which variables hypothesised to precede or to maintain the target behaviour are systematically examined in order to isolate their individual effects (Moore, 2004). Functional assessment therefore aims to discover the antecedents, setting events and consequences that cause or maintain challenging behaviours. The analysis can then be used as a means for identifying the functional relationships between particular behaviours and specific antecedent or consequent events.

One practical approach currently used in parts of the United Kingdom as well as in other areas of the world is that of 'Multi-Element Planning'. This takes account of a range of potential causes of the problems experienced by the child and factors that appear to maintain the problematic behaviour. It then focuses on strategies related to improving the learning environment and/or teaching skills that will prevent the recurrence of the problematic behaviour or provide a way of safeguarding the child, peers and staff when the behaviour does recur.

Multi-element planning (MEP) as described by LaVigna and Donnellan (1986) has four main components. First, the learning environment is examined to see whether there are mismatches between the child and his/her environment (Pitchford, 2004, p. 323). Change strategies should be considered in relation to a number of contexts: interpersonal, physical and instructional. There is a deliberate attempt to teach children skills that will have a positive impact on their lives: academic or life skills that the child has not mastered; functionally equivalent skills, that is, socially acceptable skills or behaviour that will serve the same purpose for the student as that which is seen as unacceptable; coping skills designed to help students manage the difficulties in their lives and preventative strategies. These include removing those events that act as a direct trigger to problem behaviours (Glynn, 1982). Three ways of rewarding children (LaVigna and Donnellan, 1986) are acknowledged as being effective: rewarding children for being 'good', for not being 'naughty' and for being 'naughty' less often than they were before. Reactive strategies are also included in the plan to safeguard the child, peers and/or staff when things go wrong. It is also important to consider what kind of practical and emotional help or support members of staff should be offered (Pitchford, 2004).

Three practical steps need to be taken before drawing up the plan. First should be an identification of the frequency, seriousness and the contexts in which the behavioural problems occur. Next, the problems should be prioritised. Lastly, baseline data should be collected against which progress can be assessed. All data collected should be used to support the setting of targets for the MEP, reviewing progress and establishing appropriate criteria for rewards.

The issue of ethics is a very important consideration in MEP. Where teachers deliberately set out to change students' behaviour then there is always a question of how that teacher's power is exercised, what behaviour is seen as preferable and why and in whose interest it is that the behaviour should be changed.

BIOLOGICAL AND MEDICAL ASSESSMENTS OF BEHAVIOUR

Biological and medical explanations of behaviour theorise problems as emanating from within the individuals themselves. Difficult or challenging behaviour, from a medical perspective, is the result of an underlying condition, disease or dysfunction which an individual has and which requires treatment. A behaviour problem is seen as an inherent characteristic of an individual. However, because behaviour is also located within a social context, establishing the existence of a condition or disease of 'difficult behaviour' or 'emotional disorder' as relating to the individual alone and not to the context in which it occurs is fraught with problems.

Two biologically and medically based understandings of behaviour are attention deficit/hyperactivity disorder (AD/HD) and autism.

ATTENTION DEFICIT/HYPERACTIVITY DISORDER

As Norwich *et al.* (2002) note, there are differences in the reported incidence of AD/HD internationally. In particular regions of the United States, up to 9 per cent of children were identified as having AD/HD, while only 0.007 per cent of children were identified in the United Kingdom. In Britain and Europe, the tradition has been 'to use the diagnostic systems of the International Classification of Diseases (ICD) published by the World Health Organisation' (p. 13) and to assume a 'hyperkinetic disorder'. There is a strict requirement for 'pervasiveness and persistence'. This means that behaviour which is seen largely in one context only does not constitute grounds for a diagnosis. The criteria for diagnosis in the ICD-10 manual, for example, are that the child should have demonstrated abnormality of attention and activity at home and at school or nursery, for the age and developmental level of the child. The 'directly observed abnormalities of attention or activity' must be 'excessive for the child's age and developmental level'. The child should 'not meet criteria for pervasive development disorder, mania, depressive or anxiety the difficulties should have begun "before the age of 6 years" should last "at least 6 months". The child should have a measured "IQ above 50"' (World Health Organisation, 1990).

While checklists of behaviour are an expedient way to classify adult perception of students' behaviour, behaviour assessment which is intended to lead to intervention in the context of a student's education needs to take account of a comprehensive range of factors that influence the student's behaviour in the context of school. Defining AD/HD as a mental disorder is problematic. The British Psychological Society (1996, p. 23) comments that 'The pattern of ADHD-type behaviour might be maladaptive to environmental requirements, but it is not necessarily the result of psychological dysfunction'.

ASSESSMENT OF 'AUTISM'

Autism is also a medical explanation of individual behaviour. Eighty per cent of children with autism score below 70 on norm-referenced intelligence tests (Peeters and Gilberg, 1999) and increasingly severe general learning difficulties are correlated with an increasing occurrence of autism (Jordan, 1999). Sheehy (2004), therefore, notes difficulty in separating out the effects of autism from those of profound difficulties in learning.

As Klin *et al.* (2000, p. 163) comment, 'There are no biological markers in the identification of' autism, despite advances in neuroscience. Hence a profile of symptoms and characteristics of autistic behaviour with agreed diagnostic criteria is used to identify autism in young people. The International Statistical Classification of Diseases – ICD-10 (World Health Organisation, Geneva, 1992) is commonly used in Europe.

In the ICD-10 (1992, F84.0), autism is described as a disorder that is 'pervasive' and 'developmental', and that is identified through 'abnormal and/or impaired development' that is evident before 3 years of age and by particular 'abnormal functioning' in social inter- action, communication and 'restricted, repetitive behaviour'. Boys are affected three to four times more often than girls. Impairments 'in reciprocal social interaction' which manifest as 'an inadequate appreciation of socio-emotional cues' are always present. Impairments in communications include a 'lack of social usage of whatever language skills are present', as well as poorly developed 'make-believe and social imitative play'. During conversations, the ability to synchronise personal responses to the utterances of others is impaired as well as the ability to respond with feeling to other people's overtures. Autism is also said to be characterised by 'restricted, repetitive, and stereotyped patterns of behaviour, inter- ests, and activities' that are demonstrated by 'a tendency to impose rigidity and routine on a wide range of aspects of day-to-day functioning'.

Another diagnostic tool, the Autism Diagnostic Interview- Revised (ADI-R; Rutter *et al.*, 2003; Le Couteur *et al.*, 2003), is a semi-structured interview used to assess behaviours related to autism or Autistic Spectrum Disorders. This tool is based on both the ICD- 10 criteria for autism and pervasive developmental disorders and the American Psychiatric Association's *Diagnostic and Statistical Manual of Mental Disorders* (DSM-IV) (1994) that lists criteria for autism which are similar to those in the ICD-10. The ADI-R contains questions about children's early development, communication, social interaction and patterns of behaviours. The ADI-R yields scores for current behaviours and history. A classification of autism is given when scores in all three domains of communication, social interac- tion, and patterns of behaviour meet or exceed the specified thresh- old scores and also when behaviour patterns characteristic of autism are evident by the age of 3.

ASSESSMENT OF VISUAL IMPAIRMENT

Visual impairment (VI) is a general term that indicates a continuum of sight loss (Mason *et al.*, 1997). Total blindness is extremely rare.

A standard eye chart is used to test visual acuity. One eye is covered at a time and the vision of each eye is recorded separately, as well as both eyes together. The most common chart is the Snellen eye chart, originally devised by a Dutch Ophthalmologist, Dr Hermann Snellen, in 1862. This chart has a series of letters or letters and numbers, with the largest at the top. As the person being tested reads down the chart, the letters gradually become smaller. Many other versions of this chart are used for people who cannot read the alphabet.

In the Snellen fraction 20/20, the top number represents the test distance, 20 feet. The lower number represents the distance that the average eye can see the letters on a particular line of the eye chart. So, 20/20 means that the eye being tested can read a certain size letter when it is 20 feet away. If a person sees 20/40, at 20 feet from the chart she/he can read letters that a person with 20/20 vision could read from 40 feet away. Originally, Snellen worked in feet but later (in 1875) he changed from using feet to metres (from 20/20 to 6/6 respectively). Currently, the 20-foot distance continues to be used in the United States, but 6 metres is used in Britain.

Although the Snellen fractions are measures of sharpness of sight in relation to identifying letters or symbols with high contrast at a specified distance, they tell us nothing about the quality of vision in general, for example the ability to see larger objects and objects with poor contrast – or, indeed, whether vision is more or less efficient when using both eyes together (Strouse Watt, 2003).

A clinical assessment of vision usually focuses on four aspects: distance, near, field and colour vision (Mason, 2001). However, this clinical assessment identifies only what a child can or cannot see. Pupils with the same eye condition may have very different strengths and needs from each other as people. Children and young people with VI are individuals with different interests, background experiences and so on, as well as differing degrees of useful vision (Miller and Ockleford, 2005). As in other areas of special educational needs in schools, a whole range of information is needed to ensure that support for an individual is appropriate (ibid.). This includes the views of the child and the parents/family, medical and school records as well as the clinical assessment of vision made by an ophthalmologist or other clinician.

Sight loss of any kind affects a child's ability to carry out tasks that are based on vision. Most classroom tasks depend on vision, so it is very clear that VI can have a significant impact upon learning. The kind of support that is available to visually impaired children is therefore very important.

Many people who are classed as blind have some 'functional' vision. Where a distinction is necessary for any reason, the term blind is used to refer to pupils who rely on tactile methods in their learning, for example Braille or Tactile diagrams, and the term low vision is used with reference to children and young people who are taught through methods which rely on sight (Mason *et al.*, 1997). It is important for teachers and parents to work with the child to teach the child how to make best use of this functional vision (Davis, 2003).

AUDITORY IMPAIRMENT

A decibel (dB) is a measure of sound pressure level. Normal voice measures 60 dB at a distance of 1 metre, a raised voice 70 dB at 1 metre and shouting 80 dB at 1 metre. The severity of a hearing impairment is measured in decibels of hearing loss and is ranked according to the additional intensity above a nominal threshold that a sound must be before being detected by an individual. As noted by Teachernet (http://www.teachernet.gov.uk/wholeschool/sen/data-types/vihimsi/), in the United Kingdom at least, for educational purposes, 'pupils are regarded as having a hearing impairment if they require hearing aids, adaptations to their environment and/or particular teaching strategies in order to follow the curriculum'.

ASSESSMENT OF HEARING

There is a variety of tests that can be used to find out how much hearing a child has. The tests used will depend on the child's age and stage of development. It is possible to test the hearing of all children from birth onwards. Screening tests are normally done first to see if it is likely that there is a hearing loss and the child needs to be referred to an audiologist. The audiologist will then perform more detailed tests to build up an accurate picture of the child's hearing.

Since 2006, babies have been screened to test their hearing within a few days of their birth. Babies 'begin to develop language and communication from their earliest months', so early screening means that 'much can be done to positively support and encourage that development [...] when early identification of deafness is combined with effective early intervention, with parents and professionals working together, language outcomes for deaf children can be similar to those for hearing children.

(NDCS, 2010, p. 6)

For children of school age, hearing is usually measured using behavioural tests using pure tones. The sounds come through headphones and each time a child hears a sound they respond by moving an object, pressing a button or saying 'yes'.

QUANTIFICATION OF HEARING LOSS

Hearing sensitivity varies according to the frequency of sounds. To take this into account, hearing sensitivity can be measured for a range of frequencies and plotted on an audiogram. Hearing sensitivity is judged by the quietest sound that a human can detect, called the hearing threshold, in other words, the quietest sound to which the person responds. The test is carried out for sounds of different frequencies.

In general, the term 'hearing impaired' usually refers to people with relative insensitivity to sound in the speech frequencies. The degree of hearing loss is categorised relative to the increase in volume that must be made above the normal level before the listener can detect it. Among profoundly deaf people, the loudest sounds that can be produced by an audiometer, the instrument that measures hearing, may not be detectable. Normal hearing thresholds among human beings are not the same for all frequencies. If different frequencies of sound are played at the same amplitude, some will be heard as loud, others quiet and some may be inaudible.

Four categories of hearing impairment are generally used: mild, moderate, severe and profound. As noted by the British Society of Audiology (1988):

1. with 'mild deafness: 20–40 dB' a child could hear a baby crying but may be unable to hear whispered conversation;

2. with 'moderate deafness: 41–70 dB', a child could hear a dog barking but not a baby crying;
3. with 'severe deafness: 71–95 dB', a child would hear drums being played but not a dog barking;
4. with 'profound deafness: > 95 dB', a child might hear a large lorry but not drums being playing.

Deaf children with the same level of deafness may experience sounds differently. About 20 per cent of primary age children suffer from conductive hearing loss caused by middle-ear problems; this reduces to 2 per cent by secondary age. As noted above in Chapter 6, in some places there is a serious difference of opinion between those who believe that deaf children can be taught to speak using auditory–oral approaches, that is, assisted by hearing aids, Cochlear implants, radio aids, and so on, and be integrated into mainstream society, and those who believe they should be taught through sign language. What suits the child best may depend on the degree of hearing loss, the extent of the delay in language acquisition and, of course, what the child him/herself and the family feel about his/her situation.

TAKING STUDENTS' VIEWS INTO ACCOUNT

As discussed in Chapter 1, we can look at students' learning in a number of ways. If we assume that students are active agents in their own learning we have to try to understand how they feel about difficulties in learning, behaviour, motor skills or in any other area in which they experience difficulties and what they know will support them most effectively. Otherwise there is a serious question about how we can know what will best fit what they need. This does not mean, of course, that we have to provide everything a student asks for in a school.

The assessment of students' perceptions of, and feelings about, their own behaviour depends on very finely tuned listening skills as well as suspension of judgmental responses on the part of professionals. In terms of practice it is important to recognise that 'children will make decisions about people they can talk to and trust, and those they cannot' (Gersch, 1995, p. 48).

Some pupils, of course, find it much more difficult to communicate than others. Difficulties in accessing information, communication, sensory impairment, mobility and relationship building might make meaningful discussion with some young people problematic. For example, the communication of students with profound and multiple learning disabilities and involving reflexes, actions, sounds and facial expression needs to be carefully observed and interpreted by the various people who know those pupils the best (Porter *et al.*, 2001). Preece (2002), working with autistic children discusses how inflexible thought processes, lack of personal insight and dislike of change inhibit some children from participating in meaningful discussion of their ideas. For those young people who cannot express themselves verbally, but for whom pictures and symbols are meaningful and who can understand what is going on, a variety of powerful and useful tools have been developed to attempt to elicit their views. These include the use of cue cards (Lewis, 2002, p. 114) that can act 'as prompts for ideas about [...] people, talk, setting (indoor/outdoor variants), feelings and consequences about the particular event under discussion [...] that can convey meaning in a neutral way'. In a similar way, 'Talking Mats' (Cameron and Murphy, 2002) can enable children who experience difficulties in verbal expression to express their views by moving symbols about on mats.

ENGAGING WITH PARENTS' OR CARERS' PERSPECTIVES

In a number of different countries across the world there is a formal acceptance that parents and carers have the right to know about decisions taken in schools in relation to their children, and that they themselves are, potentially, an important source of additional support in addressing difficulties in learning and/or behaviour experienced by young people. This right is enshrined in law in England for example where, under the terms of the 1996 Education Act, parents and/or carers should be consulted at every stage of decision-making. The 'Special Educational Needs (SEN) – A guide for parents and carers' (DCSF, 2009, p. 5) states that the views of parents and families should be taken into and that they should be consulted about all the decisions affecting the child.

However, entitlement in law in not always synonymous with entitlement in practice. Schools have a lot of power to affect the lives of children and their families and carers through the kind of consultation arrangements, assessment and provision that they make. Embedded within the particular discourses, approaches and strategies of schools are a variety of preconceptions about the ability and right of parents, families and/or communities, from a diversity of backgrounds and cultures, about the ability and right of families and/or carers from a diversity of backgrounds and cultures to support the learning and development of their children.

The recent (2009) Lamb Enquiry into special educational and parental confidence in the system concluded that 'Failure to comply with statutory obligations speaks of an underlying culture where parents and carers of children with SEN can too readily be seen as the problem and as a result parents lose confidence in schools and professionals'. Lamb went on to say: 'As the system stands it often creates "warrior parents" at odds with the school and feeling they have to fight for what should be their children's by right; conflict in place of trust' (Lamb, 2009, 1.1).

The recommendations in this report suggest a new framework for the provision of SEN and disability information that 'puts the relationship between parent and school back at the heart of the process' and 'trades adherence to a "laundry list" of rules for clear principles to guide that relationship' (Lamb, 2009, 1.4).

PLANNING TO MEET PUPILS' SPECIAL EDUCATIONAL NEEDS

In order to maintain coherence and an inclusive approach, planning a curriculum to meet particular special learning needs of individual students should take place within the context of the same decision-making processes that relate to teaching and learning for all students in a school. In addition, planning to address individuals' learning needs effectively means setting out to working from strengths and interests with due account taken any formal and informal individual assessment of student learning that has taken place. This should address any statutory requirements. Students' views of themselves 'as able to learn (or not!) make for potent interactions for good or ill' (Wearmouth, 2009). When planning for students who experience difficulties in learning, we first need to know whether the student or group can, with appropriate access strategies and teaching styles, work on the same learning objectives as the rest of the class. Getting this right will depend on accurate assessment of what the student knows, understands and can do. For some students with communication and interaction needs, for students with sensory or physical impairment, for many dyslexic students and for students with behavioural, emotional and social needs it is highly likely that what is needed is adaptations to teaching styles and the use of access strategies, rather than different learning objectives.

If a student cannot work on the same objectives as the class as a whole the teacher might want to choose learning objectives that are linked to the topic on which the whole class is working, but earlier in a learning progression. Usually it will be appropriate for them to work on objectives that are similar and related to the whole class topic. However, at other times teachers will also have to consider whether individuals have other priority needs that are central to their learning, for example a need to concentrate on some key skills such as communication, problem solving, working with others, managing their own emotions and so on.

Some students may have additional therapeutic or other needs that cannot easily be met through class activities. For these students alternative objectives may be needed to meet specific needs for identified periods of time. For example, a student might be withdrawn for a time-limited number of weeks to take part in group work to develop social, emotional and behavioural skills or for a one-to-one literacy intervention programme. Such alternative activities are legitimate as long as they are in the context of ensuring that, over time, all students receive a broad and balanced curriculum.

Curriculum planning for any learner or group needs to incorporate an overall long-term plan based on a global view of the learner and an awareness of the context within which the plan must take effect. A longer term vision of a range of possibilities for a learner that can be shared between the learner, the parent/carer and the professionals is important to give a sense of direction to the whole planning process. From this long-term plan it is possible to draw up medium- and short-term plans.

MAKING EFFECTIVE USE OF IEPs

In many countries, for example England, Wales, Northern Ireland and New Zealand the IEP, in some form or another, has become a major tool for planning programmes of study for individual students (DENI, 1998; Ministry of Education, 1998; DfEE, 2001). Although the details may vary slightly from one country to another, overall these documents are expected to contain information about the nature of the child's learning difficulties, the special educational provision to be made and strategies to be used, specific programmes, activities, materials, and/or equipment, targets to be achieved in a specified time, monitoring and assessment arrangements and review arrangements and date. In England, for example, guidance given in *The Code of Practice for Special Educational Needs* (DfES, 2001, 4:27) suggests that the IEP should be 'crisply written' and record 'only that which is *additional to* or *different from* the differentiated curriculum plan that is in place as part of normal provision'. It should contain: information about the short-term targets, 'the teaching strategies and the provision to be put in place', 'when the plan is to be reviewed' and 'the outcome of the action taken'.

Complying with the procedures relating to IEPs can be very time intensive. It is important therefore for schools to develop ways of working that keep this pressure to a minimum while developing systems for ensuring that the learning programme is carried out, monitored and evaluated.

TARGET SETTING

Individual plans, profiles or records can only be as effective as the rigour of the thinking underlying their design. Similar issues arise in relation to target setting for IEPs and individual profiles as those relating to target setting within the national context. The strength of targets may be that they provide a focus for the combined efforts of all those concerned to support a learner's progress and highlight the need to link planning and provision. However, some areas lend themselves to this approach more easily than others, but there are specific areas of the curriculum where it may be problematic to conceptualise measurable targets. These areas involve, for example, behaviour, the emotions and creativity.

Setting measurable targets is closely associated with behavioural approaches. A school and a national curriculum can be seen as a ladder of progression which children are expected to climb, with specific assessment learning goals at each rung. An inherent difficulty in this view, however, is that not all children learn the same way, so setting targets which follow in a similar sequence for all students is not necessarily appropriate. Dockrell and McShane (1993) highlight problems associated with this approach and note that there may be a number of ways in which a child can acquire mastery, rather than a single hierarchy that is common to all children. There is a possibility that too much reliance on task components can lead to a rigid and prescriptive teaching, which takes no account of what brings to any particular task or the specific strategies that the individual child uses (ibid.).

PLANNING FOR DIFFERENTIATION

Differentiation of lesson activities, tasks and resources would need to take account of the full range of learning needs among children in the classroom and any requirements on IEPs. This includes current reading levels, consideration of possible visual and auditory difficulties, interest level of the poems that are used, considerations of student grouping in the classroom, prior experiences of students, the potential range of applications of ICT that might support learning and so on. Resources include the human as well as the material. In a primary classroom, discussion and preparation with teaching assistants and any other adults prior to the sequence of lessons is vital. If we focus on the needs of those pupils who experience difficulties in language and cognition, it might seem sensible to use Bruner's three modes of representation: enactive, iconic and symbolic as a general framework for curriculum differentiation. Some students still need to learn by doing and require concrete objects to work with, others need recognisable representations of reality in the form of, for example, pictures, others still can benefit from using symbolic representations and abstract reasoning. This offers a clear justification for stating that good use of practical resources can make lessons interactive and motivational for children.

CONCLUSION

Assessment should be viewed as a tool that supports learning and not simply as a politically expedient solution to perceived concerns about standards and ways to make schools accountable to parents, families and society as a whole (ATL, 1996). A constructive and positive approach to assessment begins with an evaluation of the learning environment and considerations of how to modify to enhance behaviour and learning. The approach then continues if necessary with a greater focus on understanding the individual student as behaving 'normally' and actively engaged in making sense of the situation in which she/he finds him/herself. Such an approach is more likely to empower students to take an active part in the management of their own behaviour.

The awareness of learning and ability of learners to direct it for themselves is of increasing importance in the context of encouraging lifelong learning. Assessment can therefore serve to either reinforce or undermine the motivation to strive for future achievement. Students' sense of themselves as having the potential to be effective in the community of practice of learners may be constructed and/or constrained by the forms of assessment that are used with them. Assessment therefore must aim to build on students' experiences and identities and not marginalise or destroy them (Wearmouth, 2009). Assessment that is ongoing, continuous and formative and provides teachers with formal and informal opportunities to notice what is happening during learning activities, recognise where the learning of individuals and groups of students is going and how they as the teacher can help take that learning further is likely to lead to positive learning gains (Assessment Reform Group, 1999). This process begins by ensuring students receive appropriate learning goals and are engaged in interactive conversations throughout their learning activities.

8

THE WIDER CHILDREN'S WORKFORCE ASSOCIATED WITH SPECIAL EDUCATIONAL NEEDS PROVISION

INTRODUCTION

The probability that a student and his or her family will be involved with other agencies in addition to the school often depends on the complexity and severity of the difficulty with more complex and severe difficulties (as well as some medical conditions associated with learning problems) generally being identified before school age. The difficulties experienced by particular students vary and it may be impossible for families or schools to sort out the complex interaction of factors which produce or result in a learning difficulty without the involvement of others. For teachers, parents and families, knowing when and how to interact with the vast array of professionals, inside and outside the school, who may become involved with a particular child is very important to the student's welfare and progress, albeit confusing and time consuming on occasions. This chapter will first outline the range of people who might be expected to have an interest in supporting children who experience some sort of difficulty, and their likely role: the special educational needs (SEN) co-ordinator, teaching assistants (TAs), parents and families, outside agencies and so on.

It will go on to discuss challenges in relation to this kind of partnership work – with examples of what can happen in practice. This discussion will include issues of planning as well as what might be considered examples of good practice.

IN-CLASS SUPPORT ARRANGEMENTS

The use of support staff in the classroom to assist students who experience some kind of difficulty in learning or physical disability is common practice in many schools these days. The 'core' team in the classroom is usually the class teacher and one or more TAs who, overwhelmingly, tend to be female. The responsibility for student–adult interactions in classrooms, together with oversight of support staff's work with individual students, legally belongs to teachers. TAs, for example, cannot, legally, be in loco parentis (in the place of a parent) in the same way as a teacher can. Funding in-class support is an expensive option for schools. It was always inevitable, therefore, that the effectiveness of this kind of provision would come under great scrutiny as demands for accountability in education have grown.

TAs and other support staff – 'paraprofessionals' – are part of a large workforce in schools. The rapid expansion in numbers of TAs has shifted the focus of TAs' work from simply preparing resources, general assistance, clearing up, student welfare and so on, to duties much more clearly focused on student learning and achievement (Wearmouth, 2009). A second adult in the classroom can, as Lorenz (1998) comments, increase the child/adult ratio, make time to listen to students and their point of view and thus increase the amount of positive attention available to students. She/he can also be responsible for giving regular praise and encouragement to particular students while the class teacher takes responsibility for the learning programme, intervene early where misbehaviour is developing and nip problems in the bud and give individual children space to calm down without disrupting the class. New TA roles have been introduced, for example 'learning mentor' in some schools. Funds have been made available through specific government initiatives. One implication of this is that sustaining the roles of paid support staff such as TAs rests on continuation of central government funding. At present the future does not look too rosy in this area. A recent report (Blatchford et al., 2009) seems to indicate that the presence of a greater number of support staff in classrooms does not necessarily result in greater progress of children who experience special needs of some kind.

The Ofsted review team (2010) found that when a child was identified as having SEN at School Action level, this usually led to some additional help from within the school. When a child was identified as having SEN at School Action Plus, or especially with a statement, this usually led to the allocation of further additional resources from within and outside the school. However, inspectors found that this additional provision was often not of good quality and did not lead to significantly better outcomes for the child or young person. For pupils identified for support at School Action level, the additional provision was often making up for poor whole-class teaching or pastoral support. Even for pupils at School Action Plus level and with statements, the provision was often not meeting their needs effectively, either because it was not appropriate or not of good quality or both.

Most schools employ assistants in classrooms but their roles vary. They may, or may not, have some formal training. Infant and primary teachers may well also have the help of a Nursery Nurse who may be trained in language and number skills and in social and moral education or qualified classroom assistant, at least for some of the time. Special Support Assistants/Special Attachment Welfare Assistants/Special Individual Teachers (SITs) may be employed in some schools to support children on Statements of SEN arising from the Special Needs Code of Practice. SITs are trained teachers allocated to statemented children. Special Teacher Assistants are trained to work alongside teachers in classrooms, focusing on key curriculum areas such as mathematics and English. In some schools, individual governors are assigned to different classes and make visits to familiarise themselves with classroom life and routines. In many schools, parents come in to assist teachers in classrooms. Schools should have clear policies for parental involvement and may have a teacher with responsibility for partnership with parents.

EFFECTIVE USE OF SUPPORT STAFF IN CLASSROOMS

Ideally partnerships between teachers and support staff should be built on a foundation of mutual respect and trust and a common understanding of how to address the difficulties in learning that some students might face. Having said this, positive relationships are not created automatically. They often develop out of accommodations made by all parties as they negotiate their ways of working and establish their working relationships. The potential for clashes inherent in a situation where, traditionally and conventionally, one professional has been seen to be in control by him/herself is clear. If the adults are not in close agreement, or do not get on, students will play one off against another. Students often have a strong sense of where power and control lies in the classroom and of fairness.

Cremin *et al.* (2003) comment that having TAs in a classroom does not necessarily lead to improved learning and behaviour for students. Balshaw's (1991) description of learning support assistants (LSAs), for example, as potentially being 'overgrown students', 'piggy in the middle', 'spies in the classroom' or 'dogsbodies' illustrates how things can go seriously wrong and an implied lack of respect that is unhealthy for everyone. Situations where LSAs are treated like children are likely to result in low status for those LSAs among the students. LSAs can find themselves in a 'go-between' role if the teacher assumes that responsibility for the learning and behaviour of particular students lies with them. For example, where work expected of the student is far too difficult, easy or otherwise inappropriate, and there is no direct communication or discussion between student and teacher, the LSAs may find themselves shuttling to and fro, overburdened with messages and task and unsupported. Either students or teachers can feel themselves spied upon if there is little trust in classroom relationships, or where the LSAs cannot maintain an appropriate sense of balance in their responsibilities to teachers and individual students.

Effective use of staff and their skills can often depend on how the team is organised. Cremin *et al.* (2003) describe 'room management', an approach that emphasises the need for clarity of roles among adults that are defined by looking first at the roles that teachers usually carry out on their own and then determining which of these it is appropriate for others to perform. They also discuss 'zoning', that is, dividing the classroom into learning zones where the teacher takes responsibility for the learning and activities of students in one zone, and the TA for the rest.

ISSUES IN INTER-AGENCY COLLABORATION

The concept of 'special educational needs' covers a wide area that may go well beyond school and the conventional realm of 'education' into, sometimes, health and welfare. In the past it has often been quite difficult for schools to work closely with outside agencies to protect the welfare of individual students seen by teachers as at risk of injury or abuse. In terms of child welfare, there is a long history of problems in inter-agency work in, for example, the exchange of information between agencies and of disputes over responsibility for offering particular services, sometimes with duplication of interventions by different agencies working on the same case (Roaf and Lloyd, 1995). The three primary care agencies, Education, Health and Social Services, have tended to operate to different legislative frameworks with different priorities and definitions of what constitutes a need. Lack of clear structure to determine responsibilities in inter-agency working could also generate considerable tension, especially when resources were under pressure. The loser has been the client and his or her parents or carer. Roaf and Lloyd (1995) quote the frustration of one young person's parents.

> He was offending while truanting from school.... In the end we felt like tennis balls because Education said it was a social problem and Social Services said it was an education problem, and we were just going backwards and forwards from one to another.
>
> (Ibid., in Wearmouth, 2000, p. 192)

Ofsted inspectors (2010) found poor evaluation by a wide range of public agencies of the quality of the additional support provided for children and young people. Too often, the agencies focused simply on whether a service was or was not being provided rather than whether it was effective. In particular, it was not enough for pupils to have a statement of special educational needs. The statement itself did not mean that their current needs were being met, but merely that they were likely to receive the service prescribed by their original statement.

System failures is illustrated, most notably, in recent years, in the case of the tragic death of Victoria Climbié, a child known to be at risk by both educational and social services. In 2003, alongside the formal response to the report into the death, the Government published a Green Paper, *Every Child Matters* (ECM) followed by the Children Act (2004) that gave legal force to five interdependent outcomes (DfES, 2004). The clear failure in the system restated the need for closer co-operation between agencies which exist to support children in difficulties and their families or carers. The 'Every Child Matters' agenda has sought to resolve these difficulties by unifying the range of children's services. All local education authorities combined with other services to become local authorities (LAs). One important implication for all teachers, particularly classroom teachers, is to listen carefully to what students say and how they behave, and work closely with, and under the guidance of, the teacher(s) designated to oversee the safety and well-being of the students in the school.

As part of this agenda a Common Assessment Framework (CAF) for use across the children's workforce has been developed to provide a shared framework for enabling decisions 'about how best to meet [children's] needs, in terms of both what the family can do and also what services could be provided' [Children's Workforce Development Council (CWDC), 2009, para. 1.11]. As a result of the common assessment discussion, concerns about the child might be resolved or particular actions for the professional undertaking the CAF and his/her service might be agreed with a date for review and monitoring progress. Alternatively, actions might be identified for other agencies. This will involve sharing the assessment with these agencies, subject to the appropriate consent of the child or young person/family, and forming a team around the child to support the child or young person. The actions needed would be agreed with the other agencies and a plan and responsibilities for delivering the actions recorded on the CAF form (CWDC, 2009).

Clearly, in the attempt to ensure the 'joined-up thinking' that is required by the 2004 Children Act and the ECM agenda, in schools there is a potential overlap between assessment associated with provision for SEN and that carried out for the CAF. However, the CAF is not intended to replace other statutory assessments, but to complement or be integrated with them. The CAF is also not intended for assessment of a child where there is any suggestion of harm. Guidance given by the CWDC (2009, para. 1.4) states:

> The CAF is not for a child or young person about whom you have concerns that they might be suffering, or may be at risk of suffering, harm. In such instances, you should follow your Local Safeguarding Children Board (LSCB) safeguarding procedures without delay.

EARLY IMPACT

So far there are mixed reports of the effectiveness of integrated children's services in addressing children's needs. In a study of 14 LAs (Kinder *et al.*, 2008) children, young people and parents reported a range of improvements in outcomes: getting on well with school work, feeling safer and feeling happier. Practitioners, however, raised a number of concerns, including workload implications, a reported lack of sign-up from some agencies, for example schools and health, issues around communication and leadership, loss of professional identity and distinctiveness and resource issues and different service priorities that could inhibit the embedding of integrated children's services in some instances.

In 2009, Laming confirmed that significant problems remained in the 'day-to-day reality of working across organisational boundaries and cultures, sharing information to protect children' (para. 1.6). There were training issues still to be resolved and data systems to be improved (para. 1.5). Ultimately children's safety depends on individual staff having the time and the skill 'to understand the child or young person and their family circumstances'. Laming also feels that:

> Staff across frontline services ... need to be able to notice signs of distress in children of all ages, but particularly amongst very young children who are not able to voice concerns and for whom bedwetting, head-banging and other signs may well be a cry for help.
>
> (Para. 3.1)

SUMMARY

There are two particular areas in schools where work with other professionals is important: classroom learning, and child protection. Funding in-class support for students is an expensive option for schools and recent research has shown that this is not always effective. In the classroom there are a number of different ways of conceptualising the role of support teachers which indicate the need to consider very carefully the aim of this kind of provision. Two useful systems for organising classrooms so that adults and students are all aware of who has responsibility for what are room management and zoning (Cremin *et al.*, 2003). Even so, adults will need to be very clear about what is expected of them.

Policies related to the *Every Child Matters* agenda have not been entirely successful in resolving in-agency working. The 'single most important factor' identified by Wilson and Charlton (1997) underpinning successful inter-agency work remains the existence of a clear inter-agency structure where a policy and planning group with members drawn from all the agencies supported a multi-agency, multi-disciplinary team. An effective networking system provided feedback about gaps in provision, identified needs and resources and facilitated the free flow of information among a wide range of practitioners.

REFERENCES

Adams, C & Lloyd, J (2007) 'The effects of speech and language therapy intervention on children with pragmatic language impairments in mainstream school', *British Journal of Special Education*, 34(4), pp 226–233.

Adult Literacy and Basic Skills Unit (1992) *The ALBSU Standards for Basic Skills Students and Trainees*, London: Adult Literacy and Basic Skills Unit.

Aitken, S (2000) 'Understanding deafblindness', in S Aitken, M Buultjens, C Clark, JT Eyre, & L Pease (eds) *Teaching Children who are Deafblind*, London: David Fulton.

Aitken, S & Millar, S (2002) *Listening to Children with Communication Support Needs*, Glasgow: Sense Scotland.

Anthony, G & Walshaw, M (2007) *Effective Pedagogy in Mathematics/Pàngarau: Best Evidence Synthesis Iteration*, Wellington, New Zealand: Ministry of Education.

Armstrong, D (1994) *Power and Partnership in Education: Parents, Children and Special Educational Needs*, London: Routledge.

Asch, SE (1952) *Social Psychology*, Englewood Cliffs, NJ: Prentice-Hall.

Asch, SE (1955) 'Opinions and social pressures', *Scientific American*, 193, pp 31–35.

Asch, SE (1958, 3rd edition) 'Effects of group pressure upon modification and distortion of judgements', in EE Maccoby, TM Newcomb, & EL Hartley (eds) *Readings in Social Psychology*. New York: Holt, Rinehart & Winston.

Asperger, H (1944) *Autism and Asperger syndrome* [translated by U Frith (ed.), 1991]. Cambridge: Cambridge University Press, pp 37–92.

Assessment Reform Group (1999) *Assessment for Learning: Beyond the Black Box*, Cambridge: University of Cambridge School of Education.

Atkinson, RL, Atkinson, RC, Smith, EE, & Bem, DJ (1993, 11th edition) *Introduction to Psychology*, Texas: Harcourt Brace College.

ATL (1996) *Bullying at Work: A Guide for Teachers*, London: Association of Teachers and Lecturers.

Anderson, C, Gendler, G, Riestenberg, N, Anfang, CC, Ellison, M, & Yates, B (1996) *Restorative Measures: Respecting Everyone's Ability to Resolve Problems*, St Paul, MN: Minnesota Department of Children, Families and Learning: Office of Community Services.

Baer, DM, Wolf, MM, & Risley, TR (1968) 'Some current dimensions of applied behavior analysis', *Journal of Applied Behavior Analysis*, 1, pp 91–97.

Bakker, DJ (1990) *Neuropsychological Treatment of Dyslexia*, New York: Oxford University Press.

Balshaw, M (1991) *Help in the Classroom*, London: David Fulton.

Bandura, A (1969) *Principles of Behavior Modification*, New York: Holt, Rinehart & Winston.

Barron, S (1992) *There's a Boy in Here: Emerging from the Bonds of Autism*, London: Simon & Schuster.

Beaman, AL, Barnes, PJ, Klenz, B, & McQuirk, B (1978) 'Increasing helping rates through information dissemination: Teaching pays', *Personality and Social Psychology Bulletin*, 4, pp 406–411.

Beattie, R (2006) 'The oral methods and spoken language acquisition', in P Spencer & M Marshark (eds) *Advances in the Spoken*

Language Development of Deaf and Hard-of-Hearing Children, New York: OUP.

Bell, D (ed) (1967) *An Experiment in Education: The History of Worcester College for the Blind, 1866–1966*, London: Hutchinson.

Bell, E (1999) 'The negotiation of a working role in organisational ethnography', *International Journal of Social Research Methodology*, 2(1), pp 17–37.

Bennathan, M (2000, 2nd edition) 'Children at risk of failure in primary schools', in M Bennathan & M Boxall (eds) *Effective Intervention in Primary Schools: Nurture Groups*, London: David Fulton.

Bennett, R (1992) 'Discipline in schools: The report of the Committee of Enquiry chaired by Lord Elton', in K Wheldall (ed.) *Discipline in Schools: Psychological Perspectives on the Elton Report*, London: Routledge.

Berryman, M & Glynn, T (2001) Hei Awhina Matua: *Strategies for Bicultural Partnership in Overcoming Behavioural and Learning Difficulties*, Wellington, New Zealand: Specialist Education Service.

Bird, G & Thomas, S (2002) 'Providing effective speech and language therapy for children with Down syndrome in mainstream settings: A case example', *Down Syndrome News and Update*, 2(1), pp 30–31.

Bishop, DVM (2000) 'Pragmatic language impairment: A correlate of SLI, a distinct subgroup, or part of the autistic continuum?', in DVM Bishop & L Leonard (eds) *Speech and Language Impairments in Children: Causes, Characteristics, Intervention and Outcome*, Hove, UK: Psychology Press.

Bishop, DVM & Adams, C (1989) 'Conversational characteristics of children with semantic-pragmatic disorder. II: What features lead to a judgement of inappropriacy?', *British Journal of Disorders of Communication*, 24, pp 241–263.

Black, D (1998) 'Coping with loss: Bereavement in childhood', *British Medical Journal*, 316(7135), pp 931–936.

Black, P & Wiliam, D (1998) 'Assessment and classroom learning', *Assessment in Education*, 5(1), pp 7–74.

Black, D & Urbanowicz, MA (1987) 'Family intervention with bereaved children', *Journal of Child Psychology and Psychiatry*, 28, pp 467–476.

Blatchford, P, Bassett, P, Brown, P, Martin, C, Russell, A, & Webster, R (2009) *Research Brief: Deployment and Impact of Support Staff Project*, London: Institute of Education.

Borthwick, A & Harcourt-Heath, M (2007) 'Calculation strategies used by Year 5 children', *Proceedings of the British Society for Research into Learning Mathematics*, 27(1), pp 12–23.

Botting, N & Conti-Ramsden, G (1999) 'Pragmatic language impairment without autism: The children in question', *Autism*, 3, pp 371–396.

Bowers, T (1996) 'Putting back the "E" in EBD', *Emotional and Behavioural Difficulties*, 1(1), pp 8–13.

Bowlby, J. (1944) 'Forty-four juvenile thieves: Their characters and home life', *International Journal of Psycho-Analysis*, 25, pp 19–52.

Bowlby, J (1952) 'A two-year-old goes to hospital', *Proceedings of the Royal Society of Medicine*, 46, pp 425–427.

Boxall, M (2002) *Nurture Groups in School: Principles and Practice*, London: Paul Chapman.

Bradley, L & Bryant, PE (1983) 'Categorising sounds and learning to read: A causal connection', *Nature*, 301, pp 419–421.

British Psychological Society (BPS) (1996) *Attention Deficit Hyperactivity Disorder (ADHD): A Psychological Response to an Evolving Concept*, Leicester: BPS.

British Psychological Society (BPS) (1999) *Dyslexia, Literacy and Psychological Assessment*, Leicester: BPS.

British Society of Audiology (1988) *Audiometric Descriptors for Pure-Tone Audiograms*, London: British Society of Audiology.

Bronfenbrenner, U (1979) *The Ecology of Human Development: Experiments by Nature and Design*, Cambridge: Harvard University Press.

Bruner, J (1966) *Toward a Theory of Instruction*, Cambridge: Harvard University Press.

Bruner, J (1996) *The Culture of Education*, Boston: Harvard University Press.

Burman, D, Nunes, T, & Evans, D (2006) 'Writing profiles of deaf children taught through British sign language', *Deafness and Education International*, 9, pp 2–23.

Buzan, T (2000) *The Mind Map Book*, London: Penguin.

Cameron, L & Murphy, J (2002) 'Enabling young people with a learning disability to make choices at a time of transition', *British Journal of Learning Disabilities*, 30, pp 105–112.

Campion, J (1985) *The Child in Context: Family Systems Theory in Educational Psychology*, London: Methuen.

Canter, L & Canter, M (1992) *Assertive Discipline: Positive Behaviour Management for Today's Classroom*, Santa Monica, CA: Lee Canter and Associates.

Cathcart, B (2005) 'School's out', *Independent*, http://www.independent.co.uk/life-style/health-and-families/health-news/schools-out-487619.html

Chazan, M, Laing, A, & Davies, D (1994) *Emotional and Behavioural Difficulties in Middle Childhood*, London: Falmer Press.

Children's Workforce Development Council (2009) *The Common Assessment Framework for Children and Young People: A Guide for Practitioners*, London: CWDC.

Clark, C, Dyson, A, Millward, A, & Skidmore, D (1997) *New Directions in Special Needs*, London: Cassell.

Clay, MM (1993) *Reading Recovery*, Auckland, New Zealand: Heinemann.

Clay, MM (1998) *An Observation Survey of Early Literacy Achievement*, Auckland, New Zealand: Heinemann.

Cole, BA (2005) 'Mission impossible? Special educational needs, inclusion and the re-conceptualization of the role of the SENCO in

England and Wales', *European Journal of Special Needs Education,* 20(3), pp 287–307.

Cole, T (1989) *Apart or a Part? Integration and the Growth of British Special Education,* Milton Keynes, UK: Open University Press.

Cole, T (1990) 'The history of special education: Social control of humanitarian progress?', *British Journal of Special Education,* 17(3), pp 101–117.

Cooper, P (1999) 'Changing perceptions of EBD: Maladjustment, EBD and beyond', *Emotional and Behavioural Difficulties,* 4(1), pp 301–321.

Cooper, P & Upton, G (1991) 'Controlling the urge to control: An ecosystemic approach to behaviour in schools', *Support for Learning,* 6(1), pp 22–26.

Corbett, J (1996) *Bad Mouthing: The Language of Special Needs,* London: Falmer Press.

Cornwall, J (2000) 'Might is right? A discussion of the ethics and practicalities of control and restraint in education', *Emotional and Behavioural Difficulties,* 5(4), pp 19–25.

Cornwall, J (2004) 'Pressure, stress and children's behaviour at school', ch 20, in J Wearmouth, RC Richmond, T Glynn, & M Berryman (eds) *Understanding Pupil Behaviour in Schools: A Diversity of Approaches,* London: Fulton.

Council of Europe (1966) *European Convention on Human Rights (Rome, 1950) and its Five Protocols,* Strasbourg: Council of Europe.

Cremin, H, Thomas, G, & Vincett, K (2003) 'Learning zones: An evaluation of three models for improving learning through teacher/teaching assistant teamwork', *Support for Learning,* 18(4), pp 154–161.

CRUSE (2010) *The Big Hug . . . Restore a Child's Lost Hope,* http://www.thebighug.org.uk/

Cruse Bereavement Care (2010a) *Information for Schools,* http://www.crusebereavementcare.org.uk/SchoolsChanges.html

Cruse Bereavement Care (2010b) *Supporting Children and Young People* http://www.crusebereavementcare.org.uk/CYPPerspective.html

Davis, P (2003) *Including Children with a Visual Impairment in Mainstream Schools: A Practical Guide*, London: Fulton.

De Shazer, S (1985) *Keys to Solution in Brief Therapy*, New York: Norton.

Department for Children, Schools and Families (DCSF) (2009) *Special Educational Needs (SEN) – A Guide for Parents*, London: DCSF.

Department for Education (DfE) (1994) *The Code of Practice for the Identification and Assessment of Special Educational Needs*, London: DfE.

Department of Education, Northern Ireland (DENI) (1998) *The Code of Practice for the Identification and Assessment of Special Educational Needs*, Bangor, NI: DENI.

Department for Education and Employment/Qualifications and Curriculum Authority (DfEE/QCA) (1999) *The National Curriculum Handbook for Primary/Secondary Schools in England*, London: DfEE/QCA.

Department for Education and Skills (DfES) (2001) *Special Educational Needs Code of Practice*, London: DfES.

Department for Education and Skills (DfES) (2002) *National Statistics*, London: DfES.

Department for Education and Skills (DfES) (2004) *Every Child Matters: Change for Children*, London: DfES.

Dockrell, J & McShane, J (1993) *Children's Learning Difficulties: A Cognitive Approach*, Oxford: Blackwell.

Douglas, G & McLinden, M (2005) 'Visual impairment (Chapter 3)', in B Norwich & A Lewis (eds) *Special Teaching for Special Children? Pedagogies for Inclusion*, Maidenhead, UK: Open University Press.

Douglas, JWB (1964) *The Home and the School*, St Albans, UK: Panther.

Dowling, E & Osbourne, E (eds) (1985) *The Family and the School*, London: Routledge & Kegan Paul.

Down, JLH (1866) 'Observations on an ethnic classification of idiots', Clinical Lecture Reports, *London Hospital*, 3, pp 259–262. http://www.neonatology.org/classics/down.html

Duke, NK & Pearson, PD (2002) 'Effective practices for developing reading comprehension', in AE Farstrup & SJ Samuels (eds) *What Research has to Say About Reading*, Newark, NJ: International Reading Association.

Dumortier, D (2004) *From another Planet: Autism from Within*, London: Paul Chapman.

Dunckley, I (1999) *Managing Extreme Behaviour in Schools*, Wellington, New Zealand: Specialist Education Services.

Dunn, L, Parry, S, & Morgan, C (2002) '*Seeking quality in criterion referenced assessment*', *Learning Communities and Assessment Cultures Conference*, University of Northumbria, 28–30 August 2002.

Dwivedi, K & Gupta, A (2000) '"Keeping cool": Anger management through group work', *Support for Learning*, 15(2), pp 76–81.

Dykens, EM & Kasari, C (1997) 'Maladaptive behavior in children with Prader-Willi syndrome, Down syndrome, and nonspecific mental retardation', *American Journal on Mental Retardation*, 102(3), pp 228–237.

Eden, GF, Van Meter, JW, Rumsey, JM, Maisog, JM, Woods, RP, & Zeffrio, TA (1996) 'Abnormal processing of visual motion in dyslexia revealed by functional brain imaging', *Nature*, 382, pp 66–69.

Education Department (1898) *Report of the Departmental Committee on Defective and Epileptic Children (Sharpe Report)*, London: HMSO.

Everatt, J (2002) 'Visual processes', in G Reid & J Wearmouth (eds) *Dyslexia and Literacy: Research and Practice*, Chichester, UK: Wiley.

Fabbro, F, Pesenti, S, Facoetti, A, Bonanomi, M, Libera, L, & Lorusso, M (2001) 'Callosal transfer in different subtypes of developmental dyslexia', *Cortex*, 37, pp 65–73.

Farrington, DP (1993) 'Understanding and preventing bullying', in M Tonry (ed.) *Crime and Justice: A Review of Research*, Chicago, IL: University of Chicago Press.

Fawcett, AJ (2002) 'Dyslexia and literacy: Key areas for research', in G Reid & J Wearmouth (eds) *Dyslexia and Literacy: Research and Practice*, Chichester, UK: Wiley.

Fawcett, AJ & Nicholson, RI (2001) 'Dyslexia: The role of the cerebellum', in AJ Fawcett (ed.) *Dyslexia: Theory and Practice*, London: Whurr.

Fawcett, AJ, Nicolson, RI, & Dean, P (1996) 'Impaired performance of children with dyslexia on a range of cerebellar tasks', *Annals of Dyslexia*, 46, pp 259–283.

Field, EM (1999) *Bully Busting, Lane Cove*, New South Wales: Finch.

Field, TM (1979) 'Games parents play with normal and high-risk infants', *Child Psychiatry and Human Development*, 10, pp 41–48.

Finch, AJ, Nicolson, RI, & Fawcett, AJ (2002) 'Evidence for an anatomical difference within the cerebella of dyslexic brains', *Cortex*, 38, pp 529–539.

Fisch, H, Hyun, G, Golden, R, Hensle, TW, Olsson, CA, & Liberson, GL (2003) The influence of paternal age on down syndrome, *Journal of Urology*, 169(6), pp 2275–2278.

Fisher, G, Richmond, R, & Wearmouth, J (2004) *E804 Managing Behaviour in Schools: Study Guide Part 4*, Milton Keynes, UK: Open University Press.

Florian, L & Hegarty, J (2004) (eds) *ICT and Special Educational Needs: A Tool for Inclusion*, Maidenhead, UK: Open University Press.

Ford, J, Mongon, D, & Whelan, M (1982) *Special Education and Social Control*, London: Routledge.

Fraivillig, J, Murphy, L, & Fuson, K (1999) 'Advancing children's mathematical thinking in everyday mathematics classrooms', *Journal for Research in Mathematics Education*, 30(2), pp 148–170.

Freeman, SB, Taft, LF, Dooley, KJ, Allran, K, Sherman, SL, Hassold, TJ, Khoury, MJ, & Saker, DM (1998) 'Population-based study of congenital heart defects in Down syndrome', *American Journal of Medical Genetics*, 80(3), pp 213–217.

Fulcher, G (1989) *Disabling Policies: A Comparative Approach to Educational Policy and Disabilities*, London: Falmer Press.

Furlong, V (1985) *The Deviant Pupil: Sociological Perspectives*, Milton Keynes, UK: OUP.

Furlong, V (1991) 'Disaffected pupils: Reconstructing the sociological perspective', *British Journal of Sociology of Education*, 12(3), pp 293–307.

Galloway, DM & Goodwin, C (1987) *The Education of Disturbing Children: Pupils with Learning and Adjustment Difficulties*, London: Longman.

Galloway, DM, Armstrong, D, & Tomlinson, S (1994) *The Assessment of Special Educational Needs: Whose Problem?*, Harlow: Longman.

Gamlin, R (1935) *Modern School Hygiene*, London: James Nisbet.

Gee, J (2000) 'New people in new worlds: Networks, the new capitalism and schools', in B Cope & M Kalantzis (eds) *Multiliteracies: Literacy Learning and the Design of Social Futures*, London: Routledge.

Gersch, I (1995) 'Involving the child', in P Stobbs, T Mackey, B Norwich, N Peacey, & P Stephenson (eds) *Schools' Special Educational Needs Policies Pack*, London: National Children's Bureau.

Glynn, T (1982) 'Antecedent control of behaviour in educational contexts', *Educational Psychology*, 2, pp 215–229.

Glynn, T & Bishop, R (1995) 'Cultural issues in educational research: A New Zealand perspective', *He Pūkengo Kōrero*, 1(1), pp 37–43.

Goldberg, LR & Richberg, CM (2004) 'Minimal hearing impairment: Major myths with more than minimal implications', *Communication Disorders Quarterly*, 24, pp 152–160.

Gordon, A (1961) 'Mongolism (Correspondence)', *The Lancet*, 1(7180), p 775.

Grandin, T (1996) *Emergence: Labelled Autistic*, New York: Warner Books.

Grauberg, E (2002) *Elementary Mathematics and Language Difficulties*, London: Whurr.

Gray, P, Miller, A, & Noakes, J (1996) *Challenging Behaviour in Schools*, London: Routledge.

Greeno, JG (1998) 'The situativity of knowing, learning, and research', *American Psychologist*, 53(1), pp 5–26.

Gregory, E (1996) *Making Sense of a New World*, London: Paul Chapman.

Hage, C & Leybaert, J (2006) 'The effect of cued speech on the development of spoken Language', in P Spencer & M Marshark (eds) *Advances in the Spoken Language Development of Deaf and Hard-of-Hearing Children*, New York: OUP.

Hanko, G (1994) 'Discouraged children: When praise does not help', *British Journal of Special Education*, 21(4), pp 166–168.

Hargreaves, DH (1967) *Social Relations in a Secondary School*, London: Routledge.

Harris, M & Moreno, C (2006) 'Speech reading and learning to read: A comparison of 8-year-old profoundly deaf children with good and poor reading ability', *Journal of Deaf Studies and Deaf Education*, 11, pp 189–201.

Harris, S (1976) 'Rational-emotive education and the human development program: A guidance study', *Elementary School Guidance and Counselling*, 10, pp 113–122.

Harris-Hendriks, J & Figueroa, J (1995) *Black in White: The Caribbean Child in the UK Home*, London: Pitman.

Hart, S (1995) 'Differentiation by task or differentiation by outcome?', in P Stobbs, T Mackey, B Norwich, N Peacey, & P Stephenson (eds) *National Children's Bureau, Schools' Special Educational Needs Policies Pack*, London: NCB.

Hatcher, J & Snowling, M (2002) 'The phonological representations hypothesis of dyslexia', in G Reid & J Wearmouth (eds) *Dyslexia and Literacy: Research and Practice*, Chichester, UK: Wiley.

Hiebert, J, Carpenter, T, Fennema, E, Fuson, KC, Wearne, D, Murray, H, Olivier, A, & Human, P (1997) *Making Sense: Teaching and Learning Mathematics with Understanding*, Portsmouth, NH: Heinemann.

Holmes, J (1993) *John Bowlby and Attachment Theory*, London: Routledge.

Howard-Jones, N (1979) 'On the diagnostic term "Down's disease"', *Medical History*, 23(1), pp 102–104.

Huether, CA, Ivanovich, J, Goodwin, BS, Krivchenia, EL, Hertzberg, VS, Edmonds, LD, May, DS, & Priest, JH (1998) 'Maternal age specific risk rate estimates for Down syndrome among live births in whites and other races from Ohio and metropolitan Atlanta, 1970–1989', *Journal of Medical Genetics*, 35(6), pp 482–490.

Irlen, H (1991) *Reading by the Colors*, New York: Avery.

Jordan, R (1999) *Autistic Spectrum Disorders an Introductory Handbook for Practitioners*, London: David Fulton.

Jordan, R & Powell, S (1995) *Teaching and Understanding Children with Autism*, Chichester, UK: Wiley.

Jordan, R, Jones, G, & Murray, D (1998) *Educational Interventions for Children with Autism: A literature Review of Recent and Current Research*, London: HMSO, DfEE.

Kanner, L (1943) 'Autistic disturbances of affective contact', *Nervous Child*, 2, pp 217–250.

Kinder, K, Lord, P, & Wilkin, A (2008) *Implementing Integrated Children's Services. Part 1: Managers' Views on Early Impact*, Slough, UK: NFER.

Klin, A, Sparrow, S, Marans, WD, Carter, A, & Volkmar, FR (2000) 'Assessment issues in children and adolescents with Asperger syndrome', in A Klin, FR Volkmar, & S Sparrow (eds) *Asperger Syndrome*, New York: Guilford Press.

Lamb, B (2009) *Report to the Secretary of State on the Lamb Inquiry Review of SEN and Disability Information*, London: DCSF.

Laming, L (2009) *The Protection of Children in England: A Progress Report*, London: HM Stationery Office.

Lampert, M (1990) 'When the problem is not the question and the solution is not the answer: Mathematical knowing and teaching', *American Educational Research Journal*, 27(1), 29–63.

Lave, J (1993) 'The practice of learning', in S Chaiklin & L Lave (eds) *Understanding Practice: Perspectives on Activity and Context*, Cambridge: Cambridge University Press.

Lave, J & Wenger, E (1998) *Communities of Practice: Learning, Meaning, and Identity,* Cambridge: Cambridge University Press.

LaVigna, GW & Donnellan, AM (1986) *Alternatives to Punishment: Solving Behaviour Problems with Non-Aversive Strategies,* New York: Irvington.

Law, J, Lindsay, G, Peacey, N, Gascoigne, M, Soloff, N, Radford, J, & Band, S (2002) 'Consultation as a model for providing speech and language therapy in schools: A panacea or one step too far?', *Child Language Teaching and Therapy,* 18, pp 145–163.

Le Couteur, A, Lord, C, & Rutter, M (2003) *Autism Diagnostic Interview-Revised (ADI-R),* Los Angeles, CA: Western Psychological Services.

Leadbetter, J & Leadbetter, P (1993) *Special Children: Meeting the Challenge in the Primary School,* London: Cassell.

Leinonen, E., & Letts, C. (1997) 'Why pragmatic impairment? A case study in the comprehension of inferential meaning', *European Journal of Disorders of Communication,* 32, 35–51.

Leinonen, E, Letts, C, & Smith, R (2000) *Children's Pragmatic Communication Difficulties,* London: Whurr.

Lennox, D (1991) *See me after School,* London: David Fulton.

Levine, M (1999) 'Rethinking bystander non-intervention', *Human Relations,* 52(9), pp 1133–1155.

Lewis, A (2002) 'Accessing through research interviews the views of children with difficulties in learning', *Support for Learning,* 17(3), pp 110–116.

Lewis, A & Norwich, B (2000) *Mapping a Pedagogy for Learning Difficulties,* report submitted to the British Educational Research Association (BERA), February, 2000.

Lewis, S (1996) 'The reading achievement of a group of severely and profoundly hearing-impaired school leavers educated within a natural aural approach', *Journal of the British Association of Teachers of the Deaf,* 20, pp 1–7.

Licht, R (1994) 'Differences in word recognition between P- and L-type reading disability', in R Licht & G Spyer (eds) *The Balance Model of Dyslexia*, Assen, Netherlands: Van Gorcum.

Lifton, RJ (2000) *The Nazi Doctors: Medical Killing and the Psychology of Genocide*, New York: Basic Books.

Lilley, C (2004) 'A whole-school approach to ICT for children with physical disabilities', ch 6, in L Florian & J Hegarty (eds) *ICT and Special Educational Needs. A Tool for Inclusion*, Maidenhead, UK: Open University Press.

Lorenz, S (1998) *Effective In-Class Support*, London: David Fulton.

Lunzer, EA & Gardner, WK (1979) *The Effective Use of Reading*, London: Heinemann Educational.

Macfarlane, A (1997) 'The Hikairo rationale: Teaching students with emotional and behavioural difficulties; A bicultural approach', *Waikato Journal of Education*, 3, pp 135–168, Hamilton, New Zealand.

Macfarlane, A (2000a) 'Māori perspectives on development', in L Bird & W Drewery (eds) *Human Development in Aotearoa: A Journey Through Life*, Auckland: McGraw-Hill.

Macfarlane, A (2000b, 2nd edition) 'The value of Māori ecologies in special education', in D Fraser, R Moltzen, & K Ryba (eds) *Learners with Special Needs in Aotearoa New Zealand*, Palmerston North, New Zealand: Dunmore Press.

Mair, M (1988) 'Psychology as storytelling', *International Journal of Personal Construct Psychology*, 1, pp 125–132.

Maslow, A (1943) 'A theory of human motivation', *Psychological Review*, 50(4), pp 370–396.

Mason, H (2001) *Visual Impairment*, Tamworth, UK: NASEN.

Mason, H, McCall, S, Arter, C, McLinden, M, & Stone, J (1997) *Visual Impairment: Access to Education for Children and Young People*, London: David Fulton.

McDermott, RP (1999) 'On becoming labelled – the story of Adam', in P Murphy (ed.) *Learners, Learning and Assessment*, London: Paul Chapman.

McLeod, J (1998, 2nd edition) *An Introduction to Counselling*, Buckingham, UK: Open University Press.

Mehan, H (1996) 'The politics of representation', in S Chaiklin & J Lave (eds) *Understanding Practice: Perspectives on Activity and Context*, Cambridge: Cambridge University Press.

Meichenbaum, D & Turk, D (1976) 'The cognitive-behavioural management of anxiety, anger and pain', in PO Davidson (ed.) *The Behavioural Management of Anxiety, Anger and Pain*, New York: Brunner/Mazel.

Mencap (undated) *About Profound and Multiple Learning Disabilities*, London: Mencap.

Mental Deficiency Committee (1929) *Report of the Mental Deficiency Committee (Wood Report)*, London: HMSO.

Merrett, F (1985) *Encouragement Works Better than Punishment: The Application of Behavioural Methods in Schools*, Birmingham, UK: Positive Products.

Milgram, S (1963) 'Behavioural study of obedience', *Journal of Abnormal and Social Psychology*, 67, pp 371–378.

Milgram, S (1974) *Obedience to Authority: An Experimental View*, New York: Harper & Row.

Miller, O & Ockleford, A (2005) *Visual Needs*, London: Continuum.

Ministry of Education (2005) *Effective Literacy Practice*, Wellington, New Zealand: Learning Media.

Moeller, MP, Tomblin, JB, Yoshinaga-Itano, C, Connor, C, & Jerger, S (2007) 'Current state of knowledge: Language and literacy of children with hearing impairment', *Ear and Hearing*, 28, pp 740–753.

Moore, D (2004) 'Behaviour in context: Functional assessment of disruptive behaviour in classrooms', in J Wearmouth, R Richmond, & T Glynn (eds) *Addressing Pupils' Behaviour: Responses at District, School and Individual Levels*, London: David Fulton.

Moores, D (2001) *Educating the Deaf*, Boston: Houghton Mifflin.

Moores, D (2008) 'Research in Bi-Bi instruction', *American Annals of the Deaf*, 153, pp 3–4.

Morris, M & Smith, P (2008) *Educational Provision for Blind and Partially Sighted Children and Young People in Britain: 2007*, London: RNIB.

Moseley, DV (1992) 'Visual and linguistic determinants of reading fluency in dyslexics: A classroom study with speaking computers', in R Groner (ed.) *Reading and Reading Disorders: International Perspectives*, Oxford: Elsevier.

Mosley, J (1996) *Quality Circle Time in the Primary Classroom: Your Essential Guide to Enhancing Self-Esteem, Self-Discipline and Positive Relationships*, Cambridge: LDA.

Murphy, S (2002) 'Literacy assessment and the politics of identity', ch 7, in J Soler, J Wearmouth, & G Reid (eds) *Contextualising Difficulties in Literacy Development: Exploring Politics, Culture, Ethnicity and Ethics*, London: Routledge.

National Assembly of Wales (NAW) (2004) *Special Educational Needs Code of Practice*, Cardiff: NAW.

National Autistic Society (2004) http://www.autism.org.uk/about-autism/autism-and-asperger-syndrome-an-introduction.aspx

National Deaf Children's Society (NDCS) (2008) *Acoustics Toolkit*, London: NDCS.

National Council for Educational Technology (NCET) (1995) *Access Technology: Making the Right Choice*, Coventry, UK: NCET.

National Deaf Children's Society (NDCS) (2010) *Communicating With Your Deaf Child*, London: NDCS.

National Institute of Neorological Disorders and Stroke (2005) *Tourette Syndrome Fact Sheet*, Bethesda, MD: NINDS.

Neale, MD (1997) *The Neale Analysis of Reading Ability* (Revised British Edition), Windsor, UK: NFER.

Nicolson, RI & Fawcett, AJ (1994) 'Reaction times and dyslexia', *Quarterly Journal of Experimental Psychology*, 47A, pp 29–48.

Nicolson, RI & Fawcett, AJ (1999) 'Developmental dyslexia: The role of the cerebellum', *Dyslexia*, 5, pp 155–177.

Nind, M (1999) 'Intensive interaction: A useful approach?', *British Journal of Special Education*, 26(2), pp 96–102.

Nisbett, RE, Caputo, GC, Legant, P, & Marecek, J (1973) 'Behavior as seen by the actor and as seen by the observer', *Journal of Personality and Social Psychology*, 27(2), pp 154–164.

Norbury, CF & Bishop, DVM (2003) 'Narrative skills in children with communication impairments', *International Journal of Language and Communication Impairments*, 38, pp 287–313.

Norwich, B, Cooper, P, & Maras, P (2002) 'Attentional and activity difficulties: Findings from a national study', *Support for Learning*, 17(4), pp 182–186.

Nunes, T, Bryant, P, & Bindman, M (1997) 'Morphological spelling strategies: Developmental stages and processes', *Developmental Psychology*, 33, pp 637–649.

O'Connor, MC (1998). 'Language socialisation in the mathematics classroom: Discourse practices and mathematical thinking', in M Lampert & M Blunk (eds) *Talking Mathematics in School: Studies of Teaching and Learning*, Cambridge: Cambridge University Press.

Office for Standards in Education (Ofsted) (2001) *Improving Attendance and Behaviour in Secondary Schools*, London: Ofsted.

Office for Standards in Education (Ofsted) (2010) *The Special Educational Needs and Disability Review*, London: Ofsted.

Oliphant, J (2006) 'Empowerment and debilitation in the educational experience of the blind in nineteenth-century England and Scotland', *History of Education*, 35(1), pp 47–68.

Olweus, D (1993) *Bullying at School: What we Know and What we Can do*, Oxford: Blackwell.

Olweus D (1999) 'Sweden', in PK Smith, Y Morita, J Junger-Tas, D Olweus, R Catalano, & P Slee (eds) *The Nature of School Bullying: A Cross-National Perspective*, London: Routledge.

Open University (2000) *Audio Interview in E831 Professional Development for Special Educational Needs Co-ordinators*, Milton Keynes, UK: Open University.

Open University (2005) *E111 Supporting Learning in Primary Schools, Study Topic 7: 'Needs, Rights and Opportunities'*, Milton Keynes, UK: Open University.

Padden, C & Gunsals, D (2003) 'How the alphabet came to be used in a sign language', *Sign Language Studies*, 4, pp 1–13.

Park, K (2003) 'A voice and a choice', *Special Children*, 153, Feb/March, www.education-quest.com

Parkes, CM (1986) *Bereavement: Studies of Grief in Adult Life*, Harmondsworth, UK: Penguin.

Paveley, S (2002) 'Inclusion and the Web: Strategies to improve access', in C Abbott (ed.) *Special Educational Needs and the Internet: Issues for the Inclusive Classroom*, London: RoutledgeFalmer.

Peeters, T & Gilberg C (1999) in Roth, I. (2002) 'The autistic spectrum: From theory to practice', in N Brace & H Westcott (eds) *Applying Psychology*, Milton Keynes, UK: Open University, pp 243–315.

Piacenti, J, Woods, DW, Scahill, L, Wilhelm, S, Peterson, AL, Chang, S, Ginsburg, GS, Deckersbach, T, Dziura, J, Levi-Pearl, S, & Walkup, J (2010) 'Behavior therapy for children with Tourette disorder', *Journal of the American Medical Association*, 303(19), pp 1929–1937.

Piaget, J (1969) *The Child's Conception of Time*, London: Routledge Kegan Paul.

Pickersgill, M & Gregory, S (1998) *Sign Bilingualism: A Model*, London: LASER.

Pickles, P (2001) 'Therapeutic provision in mainstream curricula', ch 16, in J Wearmouth (ed.) *Special Educational Provision in the Context of Inclusion: Policy & Practice in Schools*, London: David Fulton.

Pitchford, M (2004) 'An introduction to multi-element planning for primary aged children', ch 19, in J Wearmouth, RC Richmond, &

T Glynn (eds) *Addressing Pupils' Behaviour: Responses at District, School and Individual Levels*, London: David Fulton.

Pohlschmidt, M & Meadowcroft, R (2010) *Muscle Disease the Impact: Incidence and Prevalence of Neuromuscular Conditions in the UK*, London: Muscular Dystrophy Campaign.

Pollard, A (2002) *Reflective Teaching: Effective and Evidence-Informed Professional Practice*, London: Continuum.

Porter, J, Ouvry, C, Morgan, M, & Downs, C (2001) 'Interpreting the communication of people with profound and multiple learning difficulties', *British Journal of Learning Disabilities*, 29(1), pp 12–16.

Poulou, M & Norwich, B (2002) 'Cognitive, emotional and behavioural responses to students with emotional and behavioural difficulties: A model of decision-making', *British Educational Research Journal*, 28(1), pp 111–138.

Preece, D (2002) 'Consultation with children with autistic spectrum disorders about their experience of short-term residential care', *British Journal of Learning Disabilities*, 30(3), pp 97–104.

Primary National Strategy (PNS) (2005) *Speaking Listening Learning: Working with Children Who Have Special Educational Needs (Ref 1235/2005)*, London: QCA.

Pumfrey, PD (1996) *Specific Developmental Dyslexia: Basics to Back*, Fifteenth Vernon-Wall lecture, Leicester: British Psychological Society.

Randall, PE (1991) *The Prevention of School-Based Bullying*, Hull: University of Hull.

Rapin, I & Allen, D (1983) 'Developmental language disorders: Neuropsychological considerations', in U Kirk (ed.) *Neuropsychology of Language, Reading and Spelling*, New York: Academic Press.

Ravenette, AT (1984) 'The recycling of maladjustment', *AEP Journal*, 6(3), pp 18–27.

Restorative Practices Development Team (2003) *Restorative Practices for Schools*, Hamilton, New Zealand: University of Waikato.

Rice, M & Brooks, G (2004) *Developmental Dyslexia in Adults: A Research Review,* London: NRDC.

Riddick, B, Wolfe, J, & Lumsdon, D (2002) *Dyslexia: A Practical Guide for Teachers and Parents,* London: David Fulton.

Rigby, K (1997) 'What children tell us about bullying in schools', *Children Australia,* 22(2), pp 28–34.

Rigby, K (2002) *New Perspectives on Bullying,* London: Jessica Kingsley.

RNID (2004) *Inclusion Strategies,* London: RNID.

RNIB (2010) http://www.rnib.org.uk/livingwithsightloss/reading-writing/braille/braille/Pages/what_is_braille.aspx

Roaf, C & Lloyd, C (1995) '*Multi-Agency Work With Young People in Difficulty*', Social Care Research Findings No. 68, June 1995, York: Joseph Rowntree Foundation.

Robertson, J& Bakker, DJ (2002) 'The balance model of reading and Dyslexia', in G Reid & J Wearmouth (eds) *Dyslexia and Literacy: Research and Practice,* Chichester, UK: Wiley.

Rogers, B (1994) 'Teaching positive behaviour in behaviourally disordered students in primary schools', *Support for Learning,* 9(4), pp 166–170.

Rogers, J (2007) 'Cardinal number and its representation: Skills, concepts and contexts', *Early Childhood Education and Care,* 178(2), pp 211–225.

Rogers, W (1994a) *The Language of Discipline,* Plymouth: Northcote House.

Rogers, W (1994b) *Behaviour Recovery: A Whole School Approach for Behaviourally Disordered Children,* Melbourne: Australian Council for Educational Research.

Rogoff, B (1990) *Apprenticeship in Thinking: Cognitive Development in Social Context,* New York: Oxford University Press.

Rose, J (2009) *Identifying and Teaching Children and Young People with Dyslexia and Literacy Difficulties,* London: DCFS.

Rosenheim, E & Reicher, R (1985) 'Informing children about a parent's terminal illness', *Journal of Child Psychology and Psychiatry*, 26, pp 995–998.

Rosenthal, R & Jacobson, L (1968) *Pygmalion in the Classroom*, New York: Holt, Rinehart & Winston.

Royal National Institute for the Deaf (RNID) (2004) *Inclusion Strategies*, London: RNID.

Rutter, M (1966) *Children of Sick Parents*, Oxford: OUP.

Rutter, M (2005) 'Incidence of autism spectrum disorders: Changes over time and their meaning', *Acta Paediatrica*, 94, pp 2–15.

Rutter, M, Tizard, J, & Whitmore, K (1970) *Education, Health and Behaviour*, London: Longman.

Rutter, M, Maughan, B, Mortimore, P, & Ouston, J (1979) *Fifteen Thousand Hours: Secondary Schools and their Effects on Children*, London: Open Books.

Rutter, M, Le Couteur, A, & Lord, C (2003) *ADI-R: The Autism Diagnostic Interview-Revised*, Los Angeles, CA: Western Psychological Services.

Salmon, P (1995) *Psychology in the Classroom*, London: Cassell.

Salmon, P (1998) *Life at School*, London: Constable.

Sarbin, T (1986) *Narrative Psychology: The Storied Nature of Human Conduct*, New York: Praeger.

Schweigert, FJ (1999) 'Moral behaviour in victim offender conferencing', *Criminal Justice Ethics*, Summer/Fall, pp 29–40.

Selikowitz, M (2008) *Down Syndrome*, Oxford: OUP.

Shapiro, S & Cole, L (1994) *Behaviour Change in the Classroom: Self-Management Interventions*, New York: Guilford Press.

Sheehy, K (2004) 'Approaches to autism', in J Wearmouth, RC Richmond, & T Glynn (eds) *Addressing Pupils' Behaviour: Responses at District, School and Individual Levels*, London: David Fulton.

Sinclair, J (1993) *'Don't Mourn for Us'*, Autism Network international newsletter 'Our voice', 1(3). http://www.autreat.com/dont_mourn.html

Singleton, C (1991) *Computers and Literacy Skills*, Hull: BDA.

Singleton, CH (1994) 'Computer applications in the identification and remediation of dyslexia', in D Wray (ed.) *Literacy and Computers: Insights from Research*, Widnes: United Kingdom Reading Association.

Skinner, BF (1938) *The Behaviour of Organisms*, New York: Appleton Century Crofts.

Skinner, BF (1953) *Science and Human Behavior*, New York: Macmillan.

Slee, PT (1995) 'Peer victimization and its relationship to depression among Australian primary school students', *Personality and Individual Differences*, 18(1), pp 57–62.

Smedley, M (1990) 'Semantic-pragmatic language disorders: A description with some practical suggestions for teachers', *Child Language Teaching and Therapy*, 5, pp 174–190.

Smith, PK & Sharp, S (1994) *School Bullying: Insights and Perspectives*, London: Routledge.

Snowling, MJ (2000) *Dyslexia* (2nd ed.), Oxford: Blackwell.

Spencer, P & Marshark, M (eds) (2006) *Advances in the Spoken Language Development of Deaf and Hard-of-Hearing Children*, New York: OUP.

Spencer, PE & Marschark, M (2010) *Evidence-Based Practice in Educating Deaf and Hard-of-Hearing Students*, Oxford: OUP.

Stanovich, K (2000) *Progress in Understanding Reading: Scientific Foundations and New Frontiers*, London: Guilford Press.

Strouse Watt, W (2003) *How Visual Acuity is Measured*, http://www.mdsupport.org/library/acuity.html

Summerfield, A/Department for Education and Science (DES) (1968) *Psychologists in the Education Services: Report of the Working Party (The Summerfield Report)*, London: HMSO.

Sutton, J, Smith, PK, & Swettenham, J (1999) 'Social cognition and bullying: Social inadequacy or skilled manipulation', *British Journal of Developmental Psychology*, 17, pp 435–450.

Tate, R, Smeeth, L, Evans, J, Fletcher, A, (2005) *The Prevalence of Visual Impairment in the UK; A review of the literature*, www.rnib. org.uk/xpedio/groups/public/documents/PublicWebsite/public_prevale ncereport.doc

Taylor, K (2007) 'The participation of children with multi-sensory impairment in person-centred planning', *British Journal of Special Education*, 34(4), pp 204–211.

TEACCH (1998) *Treatment and Education of Autistic and Related Communication Handicapped Children*, http://www.teacch.com/

Tew, M (1998) 'Circle time: A much neglected resource in secondary schools', *Pastoral Care*, Sept, pp 18–27.

Tomlinson, S (1988) 'Why Johnny can't read: Critical theory and special education', *European Journal of Special Needs Education*, 3(1), pp 45–58.

Trevarthen, C, Aitken, K, Papoudi, D, & Robarts, J (1998) *Children with Autism: Diagnosis and Intervention to Meet their Needs* (2nd ed.), London: Jessica Kingsley.

Underwood, JEA (1955) *Report of the Committee on Maladjusted Children*, London: HMSO.

Vygotsky, LS (1962) *Thought and Language*, Cambridge: MIT Press.

Warnock Report (1978) *The Special Educational Needs, Report of the Committee of Enquiry into the Education of Handicapped Children and Young People, CMND. 7212 Department of Education and Science*, London: HMSO.

Watkins, C & Wagner, P (1995) 'School behaviour and special educational needs – what's the link?', in P Stobbs (ed.) *National Children's Bureau, Discussion Papers 1: Schools' Special Educational Needs Policies Pack*, London, NCB.

Watkins, C & Wagner, P (2000) *Improving School Behaviour*, London: Paul Chapman.

Wearmouth, J (1986) *Self-concept and learning experiences of pupils with moderate learning difficulties.* Unpublished Masters thesis, Institute of Education, London University.

Wearmouth, J (Autumn, 1997) *Prisoners' Perspectives on What Constitutes a 'Good' Education*, paper presented to the *British Psychological Society Annual Conference (Education Section)*, Warwick, England.

Wearmouth, J (1999) 'Another one flew over: 'Maladjusted' Jack's perception of his label', *British Journal of Special Education*, 26(1), pp 15–23.

Wearmouth, J (2000) *Co-Ordinating Special Educational Provision Meeting the Challenges in Schools*, London: Hodder.

Wearmouth, J (2003) *Investigating the 'problem space' in special educational provision in mainstream schools*, unpublished PhD manuscript: Open University.

Wearmouth, J (2004a) 'Learning from "James": Lessons about policy and practice for literacy difficulties in schools' special educational provision', *British Journal of Special Education*, 31(2), pp 60–67.

Wearmouth, J (2009) *A Beginning Teacher's Guide to Special Educational Needs*, Buckingham, UK: Open University Press.

Wearmouth, J, Richmond, R, & Connors, B (2004) 'Multi-level responses to behavioural issues in schools', ch 1, in J Wearmouth, T Glynn, & R Richmond (eds) *Addressing Issues of Students' Behaviour: Responses at District, School, Classroom and Student Levels*, London: David Fulton.

Wearmouth, J, Glynn, T, & Berryman, M (2005) *Perspectives on Student Behaviour in Schools: Exploring Theory and Developing Practice*, London: Routledge.

Wearmouth, J, McKinney, R, & Glynn, T (2007) 'Restorative justice: Two examples from New Zealand schools', *British Journal of Special Education*, 34(4), pp 196–203.

Weavers, J (2003) 'Dyslexia and mathematics', in M Thomson (ed.) *Dyslexia Included*, London: David Fulton.

Weller, RA, Weller, EB, Fristad, MA, & Bowes, JM (1991) 'Depression in recently bereaved prepubertal children', *American Journal of Psychiatry*, 148, pp 1536–1540.

Wilde, J (1994) 'The effects of the let's get rational board game on rational thinking, depression and self-acceptance in adolescents', *Journal of Rational-Emotive and Cognitive-Behaviour Therapy*, 12, pp 189–196.

Wilde, J (1995) *Anger Management in Schools: Alternatives to Student Violence*, Lancaster, PA: Technomic Publishing Co.

Wilde, J (2001) 'Interventions for children with anger problems', *Journal of Rational–Emotive and Cognitive Behaviour Therapy*, 19(3), pp 191–197.

Wilson, A & Charlton, K (1997) *Making Partnerships Work: A Practical Guide for the Public, Private, Voluntary and Community Sectors*, York: Joseph Rowntree Foundation.

Wing, L (1996) *The Autistic Spectrum: A Guide for Parent and Professionals*, London: Constable.

Wing, L & Gould, J (1979) 'Severe impairments of social interaction and associated abnormalities in children: Epidemiology and classification', *Journal of Autism and Developmental Disorders*, 9, pp 11–29.

Wood, D, Bruner, J, & Ross, G (1976) 'The role of tutoring in problem solving', *Journal of Child Psychology and Psychiatry*, 17, pp 89–100.

Wray, D (2002) 'Metacognition and literacy', in G Reid & J Wearmouth (eds) *Dyslexia and Literacy: Research and Practice*, Chichester, UK: Wiley.

Wilkins, AJ, Evans, BJW, Brown, JA, Busby, AE, Wingfield, AE, Jeanes, RL, & Bald, J (1994) 'Double-masked placebo-controlled trial of precision spectral filters in children who use coloured overlays', *Ophthalmic and Physiological Optics*, 14, pp 365–370.

Wilkins, M & Ertmer, D (2002) 'Introducing young children who are deaf or hard of hearing to spoken language', *Language, Speech and Hearing Services in Schools*, 33, pp 196–204.

World Health Organisation (WHO) (1990) *International Classification of Diseases*, Geneva: WHO.

World Health Organisation (WHO) (1992) *International Classification of Diseases – ICD-10*, Geneva: WHO.

World Health Organisation (2010) *Deafness and Hearing Impairment, Fact sheet No 300*, Geneva: WHO.

Yoder, PJ (1990) 'The theoretical and empirical basis of early amelioration of developmental disabilities: Implications for future research', *Journal of Early Intervention*, 14, pp 27–42.

Yoshinaga-Itano, C (2003) 'From screening to early identification and intervention: Discovering predictors to successful outcomes for children with significant hearing loss', *Journal of Deaf Studies and Deaf Education*, 8, pp 11–30.

Ysseldyke, JE & Christenson, SL (1987) *The Instructional Environment Scale (TIES)*, Austin, TX: Pro-Ed.

Ysseldyke, JE & Christenson, SL (1993) *TIES-II: The Instructional Environment System-II*, Longmont, CO: Sopris West.

Yurdakul, NS, Ugurlu, S, & Maden, A (2006) 'Strabismus in Down syndrome', *Journal of Pediatric Ophthalmology and Strabismus*, 43(1), pp 27–30.

Zimbardo, PG (1970) 'The human choice: Individuation, reason and order versus deindividuation, impulse and chaos', in WJ Arnold & D Levine (eds) *Nebraska Symposium on Motivation, 16*, Lincoln: University of Nebraska Press.

INDEX